Building Men

Building Men

Character Lessons From Influencers

Jim Tracy

NEW YORK

LONDON • NASHVILLE • MELBOURNE • VANCOUVER

Building Men

Lessons from My Influencers

© 2025 Jim Tracy

Published in New York, New York, by Morgan James Publishing. Morgan James is a trademark of Morgan James, LLC. www.MorganJamesPublishing.com

Proudly distributed by Publishers Group West®

Morgan James BOGO™

A **FREE** ebook edition is available for you or a friend with the purchase of this print book.

CLEARLY SIGN YOUR NAME ABOVE

Instructions to claim your free ebook edition:
1. Visit MorganJamesBOGO.com
2. Sign your name CLEARLY in the space above
3. Complete the form and submit a photo of this entire page
4. You or your friend can download the ebook to your preferred device

ISBN 9781636985879 paperback
ISBN 9781636985886 ebook
Library of Congress Control Number:
2024947196

Cover and Interior Design by:
Chris Treccani
www.3dogcreative.net

Cover Art by:
Kelly Kadlec
www.kadlecsbrushstrokes.com

Morgan James PUBLISHING **Builds** with... **Habitat for Humanity®** Peninsula and Greater Williamsburg

Morgan James is a proud partner of Habitat for Humanity Peninsula and Greater Williamsburg. Partners in building since 2006.

Get involved today! Visit: www.morgan-james-publishing.com/giving-back

Dedication

"For the hand that rocks the cradle,
Is the hand that rules the world."
William Ross Wallace, 1865

This book is dedicated to the women who shaped my life into something better than I deserve.

Mom, thanks for never giving up on your slow and lazy son!

Sarah, my beloved wife of 45 years and counting, is still my inspiration and my dream girl!

Jamie, Terri, Paige, and Heidi, thanks for being my daughters; God knew exactly when I needed you!

Granddaughters, you all make me so proud! Strive to live as your Rah-Rah has taught you! Think of Jesus often, speak of Jesus often, and give Jesus your whole heart!

Contents

Acknowledgments . . . .*ix*
Introduction . . . .*xi*

Chapter 1   Unwavering 1
Chapter 2   Loyalty 9
Chapter 3   Commander 18
Chapter 4   Inspiration 24
Chapter 5   Meekness 31
Chapter 6   Encouragement 36
Chapter 7   Teacher 39
Chapter 8   Belief 45
Chapter 9   Confidence 49
Chapter 10   Friendship 59
Chapter 11   Influence 65
Chapter 12   Intensity 72
Chapter 13   Trust 82
Chapter 14   Leadership 88
Chapter 15   Pursuit 94
Chapter 16   Perseverance 103
Chapter 17   Courage 112
Chapter 18   Steadfast 117
Chapter 19   Valor 121

Chapter 20   Entrepreneurship 127

Conclusion *131*
About the Author *133*

Acknowledgments

What an incredible blessing to recount the stories of some of the people who shaped me! None of the people recounted in this book, however, could contend with the two most influential people throughout my life, my mother, Virginia, and my wife, Sarah. These two champions believed in me. My mom would not let me settle for mediocrity when the expectations for my life were set low by others. Sarah would serve as the encourager-in-chief of every venture where the outcome has been successful! Sarah also has been the multiple time pre-editor of all my works. Without these two women in my life, this man would never have been built.

My first business partner is also my eldest son Ryan. He occupies a position of unparalleled mutual trust. The American Dream I have lived would not have been possible without his confidence, ingenuity, and effort.

The rest of my family was also central to the completion of this work. With five children, 14 grandkids and seven siblings it would take a lot more ink to list all of their contributions. But their encouragement has been vital!

Justin Ice, Ean Mercer and David Ax continually challenge me to live the faith I profess and they represent the friction that results from iron sharpening iron. Thanks for never letting me choose the easy and wide path.

The entire team at Morgan James Publishing has been an incredible support to a rookie writer.

My editor, Anna McHargue, is the winner of the perseverance award for her professionalism, responsiveness, and optimism. She continually refined rabbit trails and scattered thoughts into coherent and readable chapters.

Most of all, thank you Jesus for saving me. ~ Matthew 6:33 ~

Introduction

This book is merely a collection of memories. These memories are about men who took time when they didn't need to. The time they spent was incredibly valuable, meaningful to them, I am sure, but priceless to me. They could have grabbed that time with other people, but instead they chose to invest in me. They invested their time, not in hopes of a return on investment, but because it was the right thing for them to do at the time. It wasn't always convenient for them. It wasn't always easy for them. It wasn't always the best timing for them. I have never been known as an easy student. But these individuals chose to carve out some of their precious time, talents, gifts, and skills to teach, to train, to cajole, and build me with an eye toward passing along some of life's lessons.

This is a simple book. My only goal is to relay a few stories that might, in some way, benefit the reader. The stories present a reflection of my real-life experiences and lessons that were gifted to me. Hopefully these stories will pass along some of the wisdom given to me by others. That's what the molders, makers, and shapers of this collection of memories would want. Use what you can, discard what you wish. But keep an open thought to how their life experiences, through my eyes, can help you learn and pass it along to someone who could benefit.

Obviously, not every person and certainly not every story is contained in these pages. I owe so many people so much. Books with hundreds more pages could not contain the role models who shaped me. For those who I have missed in these pages, please know you have not been overlooked. Your lessons have not been undervalued as I openly acknowledge they are priceless. My life is a picture of the people who molded me into whatever I have become that has earthly value. Obviously, most of them would like me to pass along credit, so I'll just let any glory gained move to my Creator.

The title of this book is not my creation. It comes from a conversation with the man who has affected my life in more ways and in every area than all the rest. Once, when asked what he did for a living, my son, Ryan, said that he used to build communication towers. He relayed that he had built guyed towers; he had built self-supporting towers; he had built monopoles; and he had built glulam structures. It was his belief that there was no tower he could not build. This statement did not come across as arrogant. It was simply a declaration that reflected history. He had, in fact, built virtually every kind of communication structure you could name or imagine. But the question was not, "What *did* you do?" It was posed instead as, "What *do* you do?" The focus was not on the past, it was about the present. What is it you do for a living today?

While Ryan told the interviewer that he used to build towers, reflectively, he then conveyed the understanding that defined a lot about his heart for our employees, his four sons, and his personal mission in life: "Now," he reflected, "I build men."

Ryan created, in that moment, a gift for me to pass along. This is particularly important in the current social climate where being a man or building men might be construed as chauvinistic or even toxic. Nothing could be farther from the truth. Our society needs to remember how it came to pass that the men who were the primary builders of this country did what they did. The generation before mine defeated evil, built the greatest economy, and became the greatest moral defender the world has ever known. The generation before that began life without cars, telephones, or often electricity. They valued hard work, basic education, and a moral compass that focused people on choosing to do the right thing.

The time we take today, the time we spend on the young people who represent the future, must occur on an incremental, yet repeated, basis. Most of the knowledge that old people have comes in two distinct forms of learning. The first is training by trauma. This is self-taught learning that occurs through trial and error. Don't misunderstand, this kind of learning is a terrific teacher, but the tuition is very high. The lessons are not soon forgotten, and the scars can be relatively permanent.

The second kind of learning is also experiential. But it comes through stories or lessons that are delivered from people who have already paid that tuition. These lessons have great value because we can learn by listening or watching, and through supervised instruction instead of training by trauma. These lessons can be learned without scars. We all then have an opportunity and perhaps even an obligation to pay forward our prepaid tuition to smooth the path for others to follow.

The fundamental reason for this book and the desire of my heart is to pass along to you the collective investments that other people have made in me. I will then have done my job, and it will be up to you to continue to build men!

Chapter 1

Unwavering

When someone offers you a moment of their undistracted time, as my Grandfather Brown often did with me so long ago, the opportunity to create meaningful lifelong memories grows. This is especially true when the person gifting you their unfettered interest holds great influence and high esteem in your world. Investments of time are a gift that pay dividends on a generational level—and in my case, for well over 50 years. Through his actions, I learned that sharing my attention with my grandchildren, the way he did with me, can have an impact that is immeasurable. Maybe you will see that impact immediately, or maybe not in your lifetime, but your unwavering efforts will not be forgotten by those in whom you have invested. They are efforts that can change a soul.

••••••••

In the midst of life's monumental events, oftentimes we can identify a noteworthy story that presents itself as the headline with a lesson that is both singular and huge. This chapter is not that. It does not have a singular story with an immense moment that will captivate you. Instead, this chapter is a celebration of the collective efforts of an old man who had a lake house near mine and whose unwavering dedication to a little boy would alter generations behind him. This proximity allowed and created the opportunity for a series of life lessons that came during chats while unloading his Jeep Wagoneer or in the yard cooking one of his famous steaks. I would often wait for him to pull into the yard below our cabin and run down to "give a hand" on the Wednesdays and Fridays that were his arrival time at his getaway cabin. Doctors in those days had Wednesday afternoons off, and he would fish most every Wednesday afternoon. Being one of eight children and one of 40 grandchildren never afforded me much one on one time with anyone. So, I forced my way into situations where I could be near this man who I adored. He must have appreciated it because in many ways, I was given some of the greatest access to him out of all those kids. He was and remains an inspiration to me because he chose to spend small yet precious bits of time with me, a kid.

H. Russell Brown, MD was always known to his friends and associates simply as "Russ." Not many people knew that his first name was Henry, but in true "Russ" fashion, he did something about it, and he did it without wavering. He was born in 1903! Russ was reared in the shadow of Theodore Roosevelt who was then president of the Unites States. Much like our beloved TR, my Grandpa Brown was an outdoorsman and an overachiever! He was born and raised near his childhood home of St. Paul, Minnesota and was the eldest of three with a younger sister, Marion, and a youngest brother, Sherm. Grandpa's dad, my great grandfather, held far more than a handful of stock shares in Standard Oil so their family lost virtually everything in the market crash, and it got worse in the ensuing depression. Even though Russ was in college at the time, he worked any job he could find—including selling headstone monuments—during those years to send money home to his parents. His life's journey over that decade-long depression forced him to reexamine his life and thinking. From then on, he took a more pragmatic approach to life eventually sharing those lessons with me.

Being bespectacled and a shade over 5 foot, 6 inches tall makes it virtually impossible to command a room full of people. But virtually impossible never had a voice inside the head of this hero of mine. While I never really heard him raise his voice, I also never heard him speak lightly. (So many of us fell victim to his powerful "look"—a steely eyed facial expression that had you correcting your behavior, demeanor, or language in a millisecond. The look was an immediate communication that did not require an abundance of explanation, if any at all.) People talked about the man in hushed, almost reverent, terms. Some saw him differently than I did. But what I felt from him was a feeling of belonging. Grandpa Brown made me feel special. He was a truth teller, and while he did not express an abundance of emotion, his actions spoke louder than words. I always knew I was his.

Once, while sitting in what I felt was a boring classroom, he strolled into my grade school and informed my teacher that I was going hunting with him. He then informed my mom the same thing. At that point in my life—being around 12 years old—school was not my favorite. His intervention afforded me the gift of spending a day alone with him. His hunting cabin at Hecla, South Dakota felt more like Disneyland than an old cabin. The place became even more special to me when I learned that you had to be 16 to hunt there, and to my knowledge, none of my siblings had gotten this opportunity. We got to the cabin after he turned over the driving of his awesome Jeep Wagoneer to me for about the last half of the 90-minute trip. I don't even remember speaking. When we got to the cabin, his hunting partner, "Chick," must have asked why he brought me along, and Grandpa simply replied, "The boy is ready." That may not be a big compliment to you, but it put an indelible plus mark on my self-worth! I was ready!

On another occasion, Grandpa picked me up to join him for a day of fishing. His version of fishing was trolling or slow motoring while pulling lures for walleyes. We did not really have much luck until finally he caught a Northern Pike, probably a good five-pounder. When we landed, Lee, a wonderful family friend and resort owner, asked who caught the fish. Grandpa simply replied, "The boy caught it!" with a wink. His fish story was just another of the many building blocks that were my gifts from him. He knew when a person needed building up. I think of this as a "fish tale" today and look forward to the opportunity when I can cast a fish tale for one of my own grandkids.

Grandpa Brown took very seriously the responsibility of caring for his family as well as multiple other families through the depression. He and my Grandma Ruth, who he married on March 1, 1924, had three children prior to the stock market crash in October of 1929 and worked together to raise them and three more during the harsh depression. It was made even harder when, at the height of the depression, he opened a little clinic. People relied on him both day and night.

The clinic was a three-room rented space where he was able to employ one nurse. At that time, almost 25 percent of the country was unemployed, and many families were displaced when the breadwinners left farming to look for work. It was probably the worst time ever to start a business, much less a services business. He traded medical services for whatever his patients could afford to swap or barter, maybe eggs or fryer chickens. He did not let anyone go away untreated.

Today, that very clinic stands as a beacon of freedom to physician-owned and physician-driven medical care. He was an entrepreneur, community leader, and physician—truly a rare combination.

Driven by his convictions, when Russ knew he was right, he probably was right, and you'd be hard pressed to change his mind. And if one of us actually did succeed in changing his mind, we knew we had better be right. He was the prototypical alpha leader, and the depth of his experiences made his judgment sound on most every thoughtful word he uttered.

Service was one of those convictions. He was often quoted as saying, "He who serves best, will profit most." This was not simply monetary profit, but a meaningful and deep engagement in community. You should serve where you live, and he proved this conviction by his actions. One of which was providing paid time off for doctors and nurses from the Brown Clinic to serve the community where they lived. He felt so strongly about this service that he included a separate time allotment for community service into physician employment contracts. He did not want to force people to choose between family vacation time and community service, so he dedicated it. He also issued free medical care to all clergy and their families and canceled medical debts for worthy or needy patients at

Christmas. In later years, the Brown Clinic provided no-cost physicals to all high school students and student athletes.

He believed in the free market. He believed in small government. He believed in the ownership of land and the free rights to use that land as you saw fit. He had watched his father lose most everything and that led him to a phrase I heard from him more than once: "Own the dirt!" In fact, even during the depression, he was a saver, and while trading medicine for food, Russ put away what little he could and eventually purchased a large chunk of pasture called, "Belly Acres." It was there, with him, that I harvested my first duck. The lake cabin was on ground that was leased from the State of South Dakota. They used private cabin rights to encourage people to help them develop a state park at Roy Lake. The leases were written in favor of the state, and when the leases expired, the new governor asked everyone to remove their cabin from the state-owned property. Lesson learned: "Own the dirt!"

Even with a healthy distrust of the stock market, Russ read the Wall Street Journal five days a week. He was an entrepreneur who also just happened to be a doctor. I have never heard of a physician before or since who read and absorbed business information like my grandpa. His strong business sense told him that value could be found in the tangible. Every Christmas he would give every one of his grandkids a silver dollar. Not the ones with a mix of metals, but the pre-1965 dollars that had 90 percent silver. He somehow knew that today's fiat currency wouldn't ever hold its value. As a general surgeon in a small town, one who came through the great depression, he did not have tangible diagnostic tools or access to consultative expertise as he would have liked, so he developed a simple philosophy for problem solving that served his patients very well: "When in doubt, cut it out."

There is a place known simply as Hecla. My grandpa and a bunch of other businessmen started it as a hunting camp. They had a previous place on the border with Minnesota on Lake Traverse that flooded, and my grandpa solved that problem by joining together some friends to buy some dirt. The land happened to be leasable farm ground on the border of the Sand Lake National Waterfowl Refuge. This place was also called, "The Holy Land," as a jab to the Catholics who attended Mass on Sunday mornings. While their Catholic partners were in church, the Protestants shot ducks and geese. Grandpa countered by inviting priests for Saturday night steaks to eat and say Mass so the Protestants would not get a Sabbath advantage on the hunting grounds. He often asked bishops and cardinals up for Saturday hunting so they could have Saturday night service at his cabin! This place is now in the hands of the direct descendants of Grandpa Brown. Seven shareholding partners, including two brothers, a nephew, two cousins, and me cherish this place. He always thought ahead that way!

He was a particular man who was a perfectionist with an opinion. Rare, that is how a steak is to be eaten. No negotiation of this point was allowed because he knew how it was to be done. He would tend a wood fire on a fixed grill, heating it to perfection. Perfection meant super-heating the one-half inch thick bars on the grill after it had been super-heated from the coals of a hot wood fire. The coals would have to be ceremoniously tended, sometimes for well over an hour so that only glowing red embers were seen. Then, the steak would be seared or literally charred on each side so the perfect rare would present itself on your plate. Charred and rare is how a steak was to be eaten. He tended a fire for two hours to grill a steak just by touching each side to a hot grill just long enough to hear a sizzle. I still flinch when I think of ordering a filet medium or medium rare. Would he be insulted if I or my family ordered a steak some different way, even if we preferred it to his way? His influence on my life touched the full spectrum of my life, including how he thought I should eat meat!

In Russ's world, cribbage was a gentlemen's card game and small amounts could be wagered on the outcome. While a penny a point might not ever seem like much to us, it was more about the pride of winning to the generation who worked through the depression. Whether at home or at the cabin, cards were to be approached with a serious desire to win. Bridge was to be played by couples, and pinochle was dependent on whose house rules you were playing by. But, at every turn of the hand, cards were serious business. I watched as he and his partner logged all of those penny-a-point games for years. I don't know if either man paid their cribbage debt, but they sure knew who was in the lead at the time. Grandpa Brown never eased up on a card game, even for a kid. If you won a game from him, you earned it, and those victories were sweet indeed!

My grandfather died January 21, 1977. He was 75 years old and passed away at his work desk. A senior in high school, my loss was palpable. Even now, decades later, it stands as one of the worst days of my life. I have been told that I inherited some of the traits of my grandpa, that I resemble him in looks and some style. My prayer is that my grandchildren will see in me the same unwavering dedication that I enjoyed in him. And I pray they remember me as a person who impacted them with significance and frequency of influence, just as I do with my grandpa.

Chapter 2

Loyalty

———

oyalty is not a temporary condition. The very notion of loyalty means that the trait is carried on through time, and, if true, does not change over the decades or circumstance. In my family, loyalty is not only deep and clear, but has proven itself to be an essential moral imperative to how we live. For us, it is the source of all brotherhood.

When one of us makes a mistake, and we all do, this family is loyal. Will there be consequences to the mistake? Certainly. But it is then that the loyalty shows itself the brightest. My siblings have an honor code that is stronger than a bond; it is a knowing trust that is unmistakable when times are rough. The confidence it breeds in our tribe is thorough and comprehensive.

Being loyal to seven siblings at once is not always easy, but we are all wonderful individuals who bring unique traits and qualities to our familial bond. Each sibling possesses different things that enrich our family, creating a supportive clan dynamic. The bonds to one another are enhanced by the common experiences of growing up together. Sharing the same household, navigating through life's ups and downs, and witnessing one another's milestones have forged unbreakable bonds of unity. These collective experiences have cultivated vivid understanding, solidifying our commitment to each other through thick and thin. In essence, loyalty within our siblinghood is not simply a virtue; it is a natural outcome of our connection fortified by time and history. We actively choose to respect one another.

Growing Up

In the northeast corner of South Dakota, 35 miles west of Minnesota and 75 miles south of North Dakota, lies Watertown. It sits between Lake Kampeska and Pelican Lake and is a beautiful rural place nicknamed, "The Lake City." This is a forward-thinking community of about 23,000 people, although during my growing up years, the population was closer to 15,000. My little corner of the world consisted of a brick house on the corner of our block, a bit over two blocks south of the railroad tracks. Those proverbial tracks designated us as the poorer half of town, although I didn't really recognize that at the time. Passing through our town was the Big Sioux River, which is fed from the glacial lakes corner that distinguishes northeast South Dakota. As children, my siblings and I had full run of the south half of town with few outright rules. Be home for dinner, be home before the streetlights come on, don't do stupid things where people get hurt, and do not embarrass your family. Simple rules, to be sure, although not always so easy to obey when you have as many siblings as I did. All of us are grateful to have been raised in a place that remains a tremendous place to raise a family and start a business.

I grew up in a household of seven boys, one girl, two parents, and an additional collection of extra bodies who found a temporary family at our house. The Watertown house was a crazy busy place. The oldest six of eight were born in a span of less than eight years. The two youngest came four and six years after me. So, for a short while, I enjoyed the spoils of being the youngest, but then moved into the center, one of the middle children. When there are eight children growing up in a home, you learn quick lessons, some of which include:

It is seldom about only you.

- "What we eat for dinner is what you eat for dinner. Your mother is not your personal short order cook." These were some of Dad's favorite words; he used them often to protect Mom from us kids.

The group is usually more important than the individual.

- When you have eight kids and two adults on a car trip, you do not get to choose when you must go to the bathroom. We all had someplace to get and an appointed time to be there. You will hold it until we stop, and everyone can then use the bathroom.

You don't always get your way.

- We had incredible freedom around the neighborhood. There weren't any restrictions around where we went as long as someone knew where we were. But often the needs of the family superseded our desires. That meant that sometimes we were forced to stay in the yard if one of the siblings was sick or when someone needed to run to the grocery store when we would rather play. There was no arguing. It was truly family first.

The schedule isn't only about you.

- Confession time here. I was the slowest at virtually everything. As an example, us kids alternated cleaning the kitchen and doing dishes on whichever night was their turn. I took so long to do my portion that my parents made me dry the dishes because my poor siblings had to wait for what probably seemed like an eternity if I was doing the washing. Remember—there was a time when kids were the dishwashers!

Pay attention.

- We were encouraged during these days to pay attention. Sometimes, this meant we were to look at what we were doing right then. It came with direct communication. Other times, it meant paying attention to what someone else was doing. Always pay attention to your elders. Pay attention to the neighbors, your immediate space, your school mates, your teachers, your faith, and especially your reputation. The lessons were engrained from grandparents into parents into siblings into me. There was always peer pressure to pay attention.

Our home was like a typical 1960's house except that my dad always arrived home from work at unknown times. Each night we held dinner for him, and sometimes, it was late, other times, it was very late. We often waited until seven at night. My mom became an expert both at keeping the food edible and keeping it warm. Then we all were seated and ate after praying. My dad would dish up the food one plate at a time, and we would detail to everyone what we did that day. Little did we know we were being taught patience and the art of conversation. I just knew I was hungry.

Our house was one block from school, and we walked or rode bikes everywhere. There weren't many limits placed on us, but we learned to serve. When it snowed, we shoveled sidewalks for an entire group of elderly folks around our house. When we raked leaves, we did it for half a dozen or more neighbors who were elderly. I don't remember feeling taken advantage of, I just knew I got to take care of people who needed kids, especially kids who knew how to work. Our neighbors thanked us generously by filling our pillow cases every Halloween. We also went to their houses during the time just before Christmas, and as a family, sang Christmas carols to our neighbors. We all depended on each other and together built a community we could be proud of.

During the summers, we had a cabin about an hour from home at Roy Lake. I thought it was heaven because we fished, shot bow and arrow, hunted bull frogs for dinner, and just lived an incredibly ideal summer life for a boy. I always had a brother or cousin to play with. During that time, we still used an outhouse and had no indoor running water. I don't know how my mom did it!

When your parents' time is split between eight children and some extras, some of the best lessons are put on display by the character of your siblings. Each of my siblings is incredibly gifted in some way or another and each had a profound effect on building me. I will be forever grateful to them individually. The reasons for this are many, but I can sum each up this way:

Tom: Born the eldest, my brother, Tom, served as my childhood hero. He showed me a stubborn optimistic side that always sees the glass half full. He has always been a doer and the life-of-the-party prankster. Tom was always there for me, like when I had to put my beloved labrador down and he was the one standing with me and my dog. We were both crying like little babies, but he was present!

Connie: My sister, Connie, is our O and O. For those of you who do not understand large families, she is our One and Only. During my childhood, Connie consistently served as our surrogate mom. Connie is the kindest person left on the face of the planet. As a method of retaliation to my dad and his favor upon our only sister, we renamed her. When Connie got what she wanted from my dad, we began to refer to her as, "Saint Constance who defecates pure honey!"

Steve: My older brother, Steve, is the first middle child. Some would say that this status would bring about an overarching mediocrity. Frankly, with a lot of middle children, that is the result. Steve, however, is the opposite of that characterization. He is my partner in the "Good Shack," our cabin at Hecla. His ability to laser beam in on a situation is very rare. His skills, talents, and abilities as a leader are to be admired and duplicated. One day, my dad walked in the front door, which was unusual. My brother, Steve, was holding me by the ankles over the stairwell railing threatening to drop me into the waiting arms of Tom. My dad simply said, "Put him down!" Steve promptly dropped the wailing child (me) into Tom's arms, and to this day, they find it funny.

Tim: My brother, Tim, likes to be called, "Uncle Mean." In truth, my son, Major, named him more appropriately—he calls him, "Uncle Cupcake!" The reason that I say this is appropriate is because I watched as my brother, who was the most unlikely person to be a caregiver, become the caregiver for our mother. During her years of decline, she displayed great gratitude, except to Tim. Tim put on display the servant's heart that could only be generated from someone who is truly a lover of people. His example was not only to me or to the 100 plus descendants of our mom, but to all who witnessed this selfless love. Tim, you make us grateful!

Pat: If you look in the dictionary next to the word *volunteer*, I think you'll see a photo of my brother, Pat. If you have a cause in a small town and you wanted it to succeed, call Pat. He is a constant volunteer in his rural community. Pat does more good things for more people in a tiny town and state than any other person I know. He has the biggest heart and gives more time than any person I have ever met. Today, Pat is my pilot partner but, quite frankly, also responsible for most of the trouble I ever got in. My mom thought he was perfect! One day as kids, I walked him home after he nearly bit his tongue in half. He had the bright idea to jump off our neighbor's garage roof. He landed with a Michael Jordan tongue out position when his kneecap slammed his mouth shut. I cradled my older brother and brought him into the kitchen bleeding like a stuck hog. My mother looked at him and immediately asked me what I had done to him. Pat could do no wrong!

Dan: My brother, Daniel, has the kind of smarts I was not gifted with. Doctor Gazoo has used his knowledge and experience throughout life to build an entire cadre of students who have relied on him and his decision sciences for decades. I barely passed statistics in college, Dan mastered them and delivers incredibly complex strategies and information to his students. He was also the left tackle for "JD Mash," our football team where I joined him as right tackle. We were a group of older students who mostly came from married student housing. We set up game plans to utilize our experience and speed to beat the University kids who needed to be humbled. It must have worked because we ended up playing for and winning the University Intermural Championship! Boom…we always tried to meet the quarterback in the middle of the backfield!

Mark: Mark is our youngest brother. If you need a joke told or a quick-witted comeback, he is your guy! He can be funny, corny, and serious. But at some point during his life, his sensitivity began listening as the Creator called him. Mark decided to leave his incredible MIS career and went to seminary to become a shepherd. It really says something about a man when he listens to God's calling. Then, it adds another element altogether when he obeys that calling and follows his Savior's instructions. Mark has put on display for anyone who will listen or watch what it looks like to be filled with the Spirit of God and to love people where they are at, just like Jesus does.

One night, my dad came home after being told he would get cherry pie for dessert. My dad was a big dessert guy. He often said we needed dessert every night because poor people don't get dessert. I don't think he ever got much dessert when growing up. In any event, he was expecting cherry pie. When he got home no one would admit to eating that piece of pie. One thing that was not tolerated at our place was lying. So, Dad lined up the oldest six of us because the youngest couldn't reach the counter to get it. He started with Tom.

"Did you eat the cherry pie, Tom?"

"No, sir," he replied. Swat with a belt for Tom.

"Did you eat the cherry pie, Connie?"

"No, Dad," she replied. Soft swat with a belt for Connie.

"Did you eat the cherry pie, Steve?"

"No, sir," he replied. Swat with a belt for Steve.

Then Tim, and then Pat, and then me. I'm sure you are getting the picture. After round one was complete, Connie was released because, as I said before, she was perfect, and round two began. Just as my dad began to wind up the belt for round two, I shouted, "I ate the pie!" I think I was about six years old and wanted this insanity to end. The fact that I saved my brothers from further corporal punishment is beyond their comprehension.

For the permanent written record though, **<u>I DID NOT</u>** eat the cherry pie!

··········

To all my siblings: If one is formed by their environment, you are the ones who formed and built that environment. Thank you for helping turn this skull full of mush into what has become me! Please take all the credit you deserve for gifting me with life lessons immediately upon my departure from the womb. Know that I remain truly sorry for all the times you waited for me, especially in the kitchen while doing dishes at my own pace! Further, please know that I apologize for the math lessons you endured under Dad's tutelage in the blue 1963 Dodge 880 Station Wagon trips.

Chapter 3

Commander

To have a command presence does not require skill or knowledge. It does require the wisdom that comes from other sources, like experience and learning. A commander is not one who lords their leadership as positional advantage. It is something that is garnered over time by knowing the right thing to do for a given situation through serving people. It is not always simply grabbing the bull by the horns at any cost. Sometimes it is just waiting for the opportune moment to encourage people to be the best version of themselves. Other times, it is doing the difficult thing of watching someone make mistakes and letting them learn the hard way. Having a command presence is having others watch you and then respond favorably because they learned to trust you. Commanders don't need to shout. Commanders lead from the front.

··········

The Commander

Being born in 1925 means that you grew up quickly. Your childhood began during the Roaring Twenties that were leading to the Great Depression. When you grew up in this era and your father was a drunk, you quickly transitioned into the head of the household. My grandma, Adeline Veronica Tracy, was working multiple jobs, so naturally, my dad kind of became a caretaker for his two younger siblings—both boys. He was also, in part, the breadwinner for this family with no present father figure in the home. I am relatively certain that I will never understand my father—the product of a broken home, a product of the depression, thrown into World War II. Then, crafting a home for eight children and a large handful of others who occupied our house when I was young. I'm pretty sure I'll never relate to that. But I can tell you what I do know, that as the product of a broken home, he was an insecure man. As the product of the depression, he was an insecure man. As a youth being thrown into World War II, he became a commander. While still in his teens, Gerald Eugene Tracy became a staff sergeant then a master sergeant in Uncle Sam's Army that defeated the Japanese Imperial Army. That experience began to turn him into a commander.

He came home from the Pacific Theater and had the audacity to ask my grandfather for my mom's hand in marriage. You see, my dad was from the wrong side of town and from a divorced family. My Grandpa Brown responded with wit and wisdom. He asked my dad how he would keep my mother (his daughter) in the fashion she had become accustomed. My dad knew two things, that he wanted to be a teacher and that his future father-in-law was a doctor and a surgeon. So of course, he told Grandpa that he was going to be a doctor.

My grandfather responded with the phrase that has paid dividends in our family for many decades, "Son," he said, "the path to hell is paved with good intentions."

My dad was focused on being the best physician that he could be. That's a tall order when you partner with a legend from your hometown. His partner was…yup, you guessed it…his father-in-law, my Grandpa Brown. The fact is that Dad really surpassed many of the expectations that were crafted by his inclusion into this partnership. He received accolades from his hometown, his professional life, his charitable endeavors, his faith, and finally was acknowledged by induction into the South Dakota Hall of Fame. He was a man of deep flaws formed in part by the depression, his lack of a father figure, the second "War to End All Wars," and the pressure of a huge family. But he was an overachiever who taught me to just…make a decision. Right, wrong, or indifferent, don't just stand there and wonder what you should do. Do something!

When I was in grade school, I could not memorize my multiplication tables. The teachers even told my folks to send me to the state school for the mentally retarded. Yes, back then it was a thing, and it was the only school option for special needs children. Fortunately, my folks said *no*, and my dad began to grill me on all car rides everywhere our family went. Dad driving, Mom riding shotgun with me in the middle of the front seat of the 1965 Dodge station wagon. Seven siblings cringing behind me, hearing the frustration of my dad while he led a litany of every combination of the multiplication table to this kid who couldn't remember four times five! The more the pressure rose, the worse I got. Frozen and confused, Dad would regroup and begin the process again from the easier ones—to build confidence—then add the harder ones. Ever the commander, he was going to drill this into me until I got it right. He never quit on me, and I am better for it today.

In his later years, Dad bought a used boat to share with the family. It was a large V-hull fiberglass pontoon that was absurdly heavy. He was going to surprise us, so he went to town alone to fetch the boat and haul it up to the lake. Half way back through the 70-mile trip, he looked in the rearview mirror, and the boat was following him down the freeway, it just wasn't on the trailer anymore. With a typical bias for action, we were told later that he and a farmer friend used an old tractor bucket, rope slings, and good luck to land the boat back on the trailer. Then they tied it back on, and he returned to town to drop it at a body shop for repairs. When we found out about this debacle, we nicknamed him, "Captain Crash" and his boat, "Road Runner!" True to his teaching, right, wrong, or indifferent, he did something!

He was also the commander of the road. My siblings and I banded together and bought my dad a new Chevrolet Suburban. He was driving an old piece of junk and couldn't or wouldn't trade it in. We were, in all actuality, concerned for his safety. He cherished that new rig and made it last a long time. Whenever the grandkids were riding with him, he would take to driving the inside corners of the road, swinging into a ditch, claiming that the "naughty Suburban" was choosing to have fun. Laughing out loud, he would have that Suburban-load of kids giggling and roaring by driving deep through the ditches on curves, pretending the vehicle had a mind of its own.

Growing up with nothing also made him self-aware when it came to money. He always had to pick up the tab. He would even get upset should you beat him to the waitress and get the bill settled before he got a chance. By opportunity, he once took my son, Ryan, to a drive-up cash machine at the 1st Western Bank in Watertown, SD. He provided a unique take on this newfangled convenience. Ryan relayed to me how Grandpa told him he had an amazing magic card that gave you all the money you wanted. Just pull up to the bank, put your card in, get money as often as you want, and you only get in trouble once a month. You never even have to talk about it until the day Grandma receives the bank statement in the mail.

He also taught Ryan a lesson on who is in charge. Ryan was filled with giddy glee when he called to inform Grandpa that he was engaged to be married. Ryan introduced Heidi to Grandma Boogie and Grandpa GET over the phone. After giving Heidi the once over to check and see if she was good enough for his grandson, Dad asked the obvious question, "When is the wedding?" My parents were big fans of short engagements as they understood the temptations of waiting. Like I said before, they had seven sons! Ryan proudly responded that they were to be married in October. Dad calmly responded that that decision wouldn't be very wise. "Frankly, if you have your wedding in October, I won't be able to attend," he said. When asked why, Dad told them that it was during the opening weekend of duck hunting season, and not only would he not attend, but it would also create conflict during their anniversary for the next 60 years or so. They were married on September 7th; Grandpa GET was present.

My dad commanded us to act. Some of us had an eye for opportunity and saw that as an opportunity to build a team. Others had an eye for potential, they landed at the pinnacle of the educational system. Other were entrepreneurial and built businesses that look like the American dream lived out. Relationship builders became gifted and successful salespeople who solved other people's problems. Above and beyond this bias for action, was learning that we do not take no for an answer. At least not very well and never the first time. Our family is generally made up of people who have entered the arena already suited up and ready to win. We are typically thin-skinned Irishmen who don't much like being on the losing side and never really learned to back down.

My dad was a 5'8, 145-pound commander who honed the leadership skills produced in the Pacific Theater. He will always be a Purple Heart-winning American hero from the Greatest Generation and an inspiration to many. He always taught the bias for action.

To me, he was the commander, but at the end of the day, he was my dad.

Chapter 4

Inspiration

━━━━━━━━━

Passion is a trait that is fueled by emotion. When someone has passion, they tend to share it because it regularly is on the forefront of their minds. Aviators, generally speaking, are a group who shares a passion for flight that runs strong. Flying an aircraft is one of those things that can either terrify or enrapture you. For those who love it, there is a sense of freedom, power, and accountability that is not matched by much. The beauty of flight is always best when shared by someone who is passionate about it, and from them, that passion flows freely. At various stages of my flying adventures, passionate pilots passed along their excitement and passions that now are alive and well in me. That passion has burned so bright that I now am determined to pass it along to others.

••••••••••

The Pilots

When I was around eight years old, there was an experience that I will never forget. Being shaken awake at night and told to blindly follow is an uncommon experience. My dad told me to follow him, and I trudged, still half asleep out to our vintage Chrysler. We drove the scant few miles out to the airport and sat down in a waiting room. We waited at our little hometown airport for what seemed like an eternity when all the sudden there were ambulance lights. Boring suddenly became exciting as headlights and tarmac lights abruptly illuminated the little Cessna 207 SkyWagon right outside the window. A flurry of activity ensued with a man I did not know approaching me and instructing me crisply to follow him.

My dad, as I mentioned, was a small-town doctor who specialized in taking care of children. We were going to be flying an air ambulance, before there was such a thing, to Mayo Clinic in Rochester, Minnesota. The newborn child we were transporting was born with an esophagus that did not connect to his stomach. Since my dad delivered the seemingly healthy baby boy, he had been regurgitating anything he had been fed. He was only alive due to the intravenous fluids being administered continuously. I remember the intensity of the crisis feeling severe, and everything about the trip to Mayo Clinic was clearly about saving the life of a baby. The flight to Rochester from our airport in Watertown, South Dakota typically lasts just under two hours. Everyone—my dad, the pediatric nurse, the pilot—was tense. With the baby and me, we were five crowded into a high wing Cessna with life and death in our midst. Once we finally landed, the pilot and I waited at the Rochester airport while the medical folks transported the baby from the plane to the hospital.

Even though I was only a boy of eight, I still remember being enamored with the pilot and his fascinating job. No part of this life-saving adventure could be conducted without this heroic man and his flying skills! Meanwhile, my dad and the nurse did boring medical stuff like transporting the baby boy via ambulance into the clinic.

While waiting, I dozed off only to be awakened by my new pilot friend who invited me to join him as he did what I presume was preflight of the aircraft. The memories were of walking around "my" Cessna 207 SkyWagon and looking at this incredible bird like it was the most capable aircraft in the world. He made sure she was airworthy and proceeded back into the building like we owned the planet. My dad, the nurse, my new pilot friend, and I were going to be heading home soon. When the pair returned from their quick round trip to the hospital, we went out onto the wind-bitten tarmac and Dad's words still echo to this day: "My son rides in front!"

That night would eventually change my life. We boarded the SkyWagon and headed back to Watertown. The notion and thrill of flying had been seared into my memory bank after the pilot let me hold the yoke. Sitting up front in that aircraft was mesmerizing. The language was fascinating, the instruments were confusing, but cool. Then the weather changed for the worse. I recall the beginning of the snow. I recall how the feel of the yoke gave me a sense of power and the voice that encouraged me to be gentle with my pressure. I remember the security of the pilot saying we would be fine in the light snow. I recall the "feeling" that I was flying the aircraft. I recall the deep emotion of being just like the pilot. In my heart and mind, that night, I became a pilot.

That feeling would remain a latent portion of my existence for the next 39 years. Yes, 39 years! On a vacation trip back to South Dakota one April, I remember seeing a small plane take flight and immediately found myself reliving my childhood flying adventure. Then I asked Dad, "When was the last time you went up in a small plane?" He told me that he and my Grandpa Brown had last flown with his partner, John. They spent the flight looking over old haunts, favorite hunting grounds, and the ranches and farms they visited so very long ago. He also said he would give anything to do that again. I immediately made the decision that I would fly him myself, as his pilot. He would get to experience that again.

On May 25, 2006, at 47 years old, I took my first flight lesson. Many people think of this as the starting point in flight training, but I was already way down the road in my commitment to flying—at least from a decision standpoint. On October 19, 2006, I rented a Cessna 172 from Fargo Jet Center. From there, I flew down to pick up my dad in Britton, South Dakota and took him on a ride that will stay with me until I die. We flew over all of the old places, we flew over the new places, and we flew to the future places until his bladder gave out. Then we landed back at Britton. It was my first landing on a grass strip, and my son, Major, was able to share that flight with us. What a gift it was to me to be able to make them both proud of what had been accomplished in five months' time following this new aviation passion! It was the thrill of a lifetime! But I was just getting started.

After getting my private pilot's license in 2006, I began to understand that if you live in the Puget Sound region, you had better be able to fly in the clouds. The following year, I began training to get the instrument rating required to fly in Seattle's typically dreary weather. After concluding flight training, I passed the practical examination in Alexandria, Minnesota. With my daughter, Terri, keeping me company, we headed home to Washington State, but the trip included a stop to see Mom and Dad.

We would have lunch with Mom and Dad on November 10, 2007, at the Guest House Hotel restaurant where I would again meet my mentor. Dad introduced us to a frail and significantly older fellow who had stopped by our table. This was my pilot!

His phrase to me upon hearing about my freshly won instrument rating was simply epic. He said to me, "Son, you're now an aviator."

· · · · · · · · ·

Shortly after getting certificated as a private pilot, I realized that our business could really use a capable aircraft. The branches of our company were at least five hours apart by car, and we often needed to share parts, tools, or equipment. Further, I could visit the branch and my grandkids without driving over Snoqualmie Pass in the traffic and winter weather it is so famous for. It turns out that Piper Aircraft built a model that suited my needs nicely. It is called a Saratoga II T/C. The backdoor had a second hatch that allowed me to fit a wireless antenna into the cavernous 10-foot-long passenger and cargo area. The decision for me was easy: Get the best airplane you can afford. I found a red, white, and blue Saratoga in St. Paul and made the purchase. We called her, "The Patriot!"

Jesse, my niece's husband, was an experienced pilot, and he would meet me to train me in the operation of this complex, high-performance aircraft. Because it has retractable landing gear, is turbo-charged, and has a higher horsepower engine, I needed to get 25 hours of flight time in for the insurance company. Jesse was amazing and patient. We flew all over the country getting those hours in. We finally returned to Detroit where he lives, and he helped me land on the snow-covered runway. He made me do about 10 more landings in the slushy and nasty conditions until I was just plain beat. I asked Jesse when we were departing the airport why he made me perform so many landings in the snow. "Jim," he replied, "you are the brother of my father-in-law. If you die in this plane, my life will be ruined." Thanks for your training efforts, Jesse, I still have the shiny side up!

In 2020, we moved to Boise, Idaho. On a trip from our Three Forks, Montana branch back home, I was over the Frank Church–River of No Return Wilderness Area. The area is almost 2.4 million acres of impossibly steep, rugged mountains, deep canyons, and intense boulder-filled, whitewater rivers. As I looked down over the place of ridiculous beauty, I realized that I was flying a single engine aircraft, and if anything went wrong, there was absolutely no place to land. "Maybe it was time for a twin engine," I wondered.

The search began, and I settled on an Eclipse 500 twin engine jet. The speed of the aircraft was desirable, the budget didn't break the bank at the fuel pump, and the number of nights in a hotel would be significantly reduced. I found an Eclipse in Michigan and made the purchase. The training started and ended rather abruptly. My initial instructor and I had difficulty communicating. It's much more difficult to fly a jet than just hopping in and firing her up. I was going to need some seriously good instruction to make the big jump from a single engine propellor driven airplane to a twin engine jet.

This is where Rich stepped in. Rich is a veteran of the U.S. Air Force where he served as a fighter pilot flying F-16 Fighting Falcons.

He went from there to flying passengers around for 20 years as a captain for Delta Air Lines. Rich is the consummate professional and was as patient as any instructor on the planet. He allowed me to make mistakes and then debriefed the why when the stress and workload were lower. A week into our training, he moved me away from home and work so we could focus exclusively on flying and systems study for extended days—and he pushed me. At one point, I asked Rich how I was going to tell my wife I bought a jet that I cannot even fly. He quietly encouraged me and kept telling me I was on track. He only got visibly upset with me once and that was when I did not conduct a go-around when I should have. "Are you trying to kill us both, Jim?" he exclaimed. Then he calmed down, we went back to the hotel, and he debriefed with me on decision-making in terms of go-arounds. The time came for my checkride, and the FAA examiner flew in from Chicago. Checkrides are notoriously high-stress environments and either pass or fail! I practically aced my checkride. Rich was so proud, and my wife, Sarah, was so relieved that I was now a jet-rated pilot. I could never thank Rich enough for not giving up on me and offering continual encouragement. I owe him more than one!

Pilots have been my source of aviation encouragement. This inspiration has lasted for 55 years and counting. It has led me to the pinnacle of private aviation as I have earned a multi-engine turbine rating and fly my own twin engine jet. The seeds that were planted so long ago serve as an example to me not only in aviation but in life. I am called to be an encourager and pass along the gifts that my pilots have trusted with me. Perhaps, someday, someone will remember my encouragement and even when they forget my name, that encouragement will have a far more enduring value.

Chapter 5

Meekness

Someone once said to me that meekness is a virtue that looks like a Volkswagen Bug passing a Lamborghini on the Autobahn. The Lamborghini has the capacity to surge ahead with ease but chooses to let the lesser capable car go to the front. It is not a function of power but of consideration. People who are meek have the trait because it is a choice. When that decision is made, it becomes an active verb. Meekness is something that can be refined with age and experience through practice, as you learn when and how to consider others before yourself.

•••••••••

Uncle Earle—Those Eyes

The eyes of Uncle Earle could communicate more than any word. They revealed kindness when he knew someone needed a gentle gesture. They communicated disappointment to a terrified child who knew he had been caught doing something he should not be doing. So famous was that look that it got its own name, the "ERK look" —the initials of the man whose look could stop a freight train. If only you could perceive the eyes that contained both mercy and power. He was a true portrait of controlled strength with a laugh that could transform a room. And with his simple eye contact, he never had any need for volume. Those eyes could twinkle!

My Uncle Earle was born and spent his formative years in the throes of the Great Depression. His father was the volunteer fire chief at Watertown for 40 years. Their life was one of little income during the depression, but they were never poor. Like many families, including my own, we gleaned potatoes, cucumbers, and corn from the edges of fields that had already been harvested. My family did this to feed a bunch of kids, Earle's family gleaned because they needed any available funds for things other than food.

Earle was an amazing athlete. He was a high school basketball star. He was a big fellow who had speed. His size and quickness landed him a scholarship to play football at the University of South Dakota for four years. He was an offensive lineman playing guard and delivering punishing blocks in a game where running the football was the only way to win. Like many great players, his intensity on the field of play did not match his gentle demeanor off the field. Here, too, he was a picture of strength under control. In his "growing the business" years, Earle took up golf. Like any natural athlete, he was good at it and became a student of the game. This helped him develop a spectacular drive that awed people who watched from the tee box. Every time he played with my dad, who had no long drive at all, he was reminded, "Drive for show, putt for dough!" Everyone who saw Earle drive a golf ball loved that show!

ERK was a big man who carried himself with a military bearing that probably stemmed from his time as an officer. He joined the U.S. Army and went to Officer Candidate School right as the Korean War was ending. In the evenings and usually after a cocktail made with Cabin Still Bourbon, he would tease my dad that he outranked him. Dad would remind Earle that sergeants ran the military, and Earle would always quip that if Dad wanted to address him, he should say, "Sir," and probably offer a salute. They had bantered back and forth wherever they were, but especially at our beloved goose hunting camp near Hecla, South Dakota.

I recently had an opportunity to look through that cabin in our hunting camp, and I found a series of notes written by Earle. The notes that I found were a string of multigenerational messages to children and grandchildren. Uniformly they expressed both gratefulness and encouragement. They were written in longhand, and the expressions were filled with affection and affirmation. I noticed them because they were on display by the third generation of recipients. Those notes will serve as a constant reminder both to this generation and future generations of a kind and grateful man who took the time to express his love to whomever might walk through those doors.

Earle also built an independent insurance company after a couple of tries at working for someone else. Because he was kind, people naturally gravitated toward him and trusted him. He also went out of his way to be an effective community service leader. His quiet way was the opposite of the flamboyant style of the generation to follow. Earle took care of people like Rhoda, his secretary who served as the voice of Kinsman Insurance for decades. In their little office above the First National Bank Building, Rhoda was a physically disabled survivor of polio. She had lifelong challenges with her foot, hand, and speech but Earle was loyal to her service, and in a time where disabilities were put in a closet, he simply put her to work. Like a true friend, Earle also sent money and helped with medical transportation for the seriously ill child of a friend. He also jumped in as a mentor for many, including that friend. His business began in 1958 and continues today providing multi-generational benefits like so many of the small businesses across the Midwest.

My uncle was an agent for large insurance companies. While contractually he represented the insurance companies, he never forgot who paid the premium dollars. He had a long history of going to bat for people in our town, especially when insurance companies were being difficult. I know of more than a few people who were glad that this offensive lineman gladiator was their insurance broker. He would not hesitate to take on the insurance company on behalf of his insured! If for any reason the insurance companies didn't play fair, they got a dose of Earle they didn't soon forget. He was known to step in to "get stuff squared away for his people." I don't think it would have been pleasant to see this man standing on the other side of your desk if you were not being a fair dealer.

Quantifying all my memories of Uncle Earle hasn't been easy simply because he was around so often. There isn't a single story that triggers a breakout blinding memory. Sometimes it is just as simple as the way he treated his black Labrador, King, or the gentle way he spoke to me and the picture that remains from not one memory, but a thousand interactions. Earle can best be described as strength under control on a constant basis. That alone is enough to impact me as a young man. And that he could do it with a single look has made him even more impactful to me.

Earle could be remembered for a lot of different things, athletics, military service, business acumen, church activities, or community support. But those are not the things that come to mind when I reflect on my beloved uncle. What comes to mind is the ERK look. More importantly, though, I remember the meekness, kindness, gentleness, and genuine smile that accompanied that one-of-a kind look. But what will I remember forever? Those eyes that said so much.

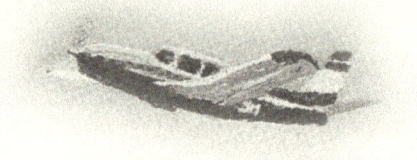

Chapter 6

Encouragement

———————

Being aware of your surroundings is a skill. One of the many benefits of that kind of awareness is noticing other people and their needs. The gift of encouragement always begins by noticing someone who could use the encouragement. While we all could use an occasional *atta-boy*, encouragement that comes from someone in a position of authority or above the station of the discouraged results is something magical. The discouraged can't help but feel a renewed sense of hope, even if only for a moment. This verbal skill is a valuable asset to both parties and works best when practiced sincerely and often.

· · · · · · · · · ·

My Encourager

Norb was, by any measure, an athlete. A lean man, he walked like someone who knew how to keep his body healthy. He was also a sports nut who thrived on the high school sports scene. His sons were also athletes.

Norb was an important part of the 1925 group of influencers. He went to grade school and high school and then worked in the same town his entire career. He was the administrator of the Brown Clinic started by my grandpa and served in that role for 37 years. Are you seeing the picture of loyalty those depression era kids have? But Norb was more than that. He lost his mother in 1932, and his father drowned in 1933 when Norb was merely eight years old. His Aunt Lena and Uncle Matt then raised him as their own.

He attended the same high school as I did prior to his enlistment in the United States Army Air Corps, now the U.S. Air Force. Norb was a nose gunner in a B-24 and conducted 46 successful bombing runs over Europe during World War II. Only one-quarter of nose gunners back then could complete 25 missions, much less 46. The nose gunner was also a primary target because of their place on the front of the aircraft. The B-24 Liberator is known as, "The Flying Coffin," because it was so difficult to fly.

Norb received an honorable discharge in 1945, and in 1946, he married Mary Ann and went to college. Graduating in 1950, he went to work for Grandpa Brown as his business manager and administrator holding that position with Brown Clinic until he retired in 1987.

I knew none of those things growing up. What I knew is that when I was in seventh grade, I played a football game that I do not even remember. Sports were not that big of a deal at our house. My folks never got the time to watch me play. But the phone rang that night after dinner, and I was told it was for me. I did not have any idea who was calling, but it turned out to be Norb. He spoke to me about a couple of plays I was involved in like he was calling a play by play of the Super Bowl. Then he told me he was proud and to keep up the effort. I was flabbergasted! This was an important man around our town, and he took the time to call me!

Then, in the eighth grade, I made a third-down tackle for a loss against the Brookings Bobcats, and it happened again. Norb called me and replayed the down so that I could see it in my own mind. What had occurred on the field so quickly was broken down into heroic moments of superior athletic prowess. It was so incredible to be lifted up, even if it was a bit generous. He gave me a gift of confidence in myself that had not been watered very much. It left a mark on me that has impacted me to this day.

In the ninth grade, Norb called again when I was fortunate enough to block a punt. He spoke as if the ABC Wide World of Sports should have been covering it. He repeated these phone calls on a semi-regular basis, like when I won my only wrestling match ever. He called again when I won the state championship in a prepared speech.

In high school, Norb took me out to his rural home where he taught me some of the fine art of working with a retriever. What I remember is while he showed me how to handle the dogs, he then let me do it while making teenaged mistakes. He continually offered suggestions and teaching through constructive commentary that was building my confidence. This repetitive positive feedback helped me understand that I mattered to him individually.

Norb was an encourager; I think it may have been his love language. He had nothing to gain from encouraging me. But this is how he showed he cared. I will do my best to do as he did and pass that encouragement along.

Chapter 7

Teacher

=====

School teachers are the molders of our society's children. They play a role that can never be underestimated as we all work to build a strong, civilized culture. And while school teachers are critical in our culture, the same can be said for other kinds of teachers as well. Anyone who is willing to come alongside someone, no matter the subject, can be a treasured teacher who can offer skills and insights that can benefit a learner for the full of their life.

··········

My Teacher

Like so many of the men who have worked hard to transform the knucklehead that I was into the hopefully responsible man I have become, I have a long history with John. Not many people get a diverse look at who they spend time with. Either it is family for a long time or friends for a long time. Neither group has much of an opportunity to change their perspective. That works in both directions. Your perspective of me and my perspective of you don't get much of an opportunity to change our point of view or even refocus. You are who I know you have always been. I also remain the person you knew me to be. Perhaps we keep others in a box too long?

That is not the case with John, as we served together in many capacities. In fact, so many that I had to create a list of them so you would understand the depth of his knowledge of me.

- Teacher—John was my teacher as a senior in high school where he was the welding instructor in what has become the Northeast Technical High School.
- Advisor—John was the advisor to the Vocational Industrial Clubs of America chapter from Watertown where he led efforts to build the trades.
- Engaged Encounter—John and his lovely wife, Lori, led Sarah and me to commit to one another for a "lifelong gig," as John would call it. It was an effort to get us to think about a committed married life before we got hitched. I think we can agree after 45 years that their efforts were a success!
- Boss—I went to work for John when he was the president of Energy Industries and subsequent to that, the president of Enercept, Inc.
- Competitor—John and I were fierce competitors when I took over a near hopeless manufacturing operation in the Puget Sound region. We both respected each other enough to not worry about whose nose got bloodied, as long as we were fighting fair!

- Peer—John and I served together on the board of directors of SIPA, the Structural Insulated Panel Association, a National Trade Association we literally built from the ground up.
- Servant—John and I both served as the president of SIPA during different terms prior to my becoming the COO while turning the organization around financially.
- Rancher—His fourth career by my count, John followed his dream of becoming a rancher with Lori standing by his side.

All these touch points are important because John affected me more than most anyone could understand. When I was selling fruit for a VICA fundraiser, he challenged me so vociferously that I ultimately sold 300 cases of oranges, all of which I had to deliver myself, in my own car, and with my own gas money. The challenge came when a broken hand kept me from his welding class. Not one to waste an opportunity to teach, he made me sit in the front office dialing up anyone who would buy a case of those stupid oranges. He never let me forget that if you can sell something, you'll never need to look very far for work.

John was an expert at practical jokes. Once when we were on a VICA trip in an old Oldsmobile station wagon packed with sleeping high school kids, John waited until everyone else was asleep. He then slammed on the brakes in the middle of the highway while slapping the ceiling and screaming like a banshee, hoping to scare us senseless. I think the crazy bugger laughed at us for another hour while our blood pressure dropped back to normal levels. He also may have used it as an amusing way to keep himself from falling asleep. We will never know, but it was incredibly funny. I have since used that trick with kids as well.

We paid John back when we set empty beer bottles on the door outside of his welding shop every weekend. My cousin had him first period and helped me respond to that joker. Every Monday morning, John would swing open the shop door, and the bottles would break. This went on for weeks until John began to park in the back of the school to combat our tricks. I never knew if he figured out I was the culprit. He did ask me a few years later if I knew about it. I never let on about my knowledge of what he was talking about but am pretty sure he knew I planted the bottles to break. He just kept building our relationship anyway.

John was also a coach. I won the gold medal in South Dakota for prepared speech at the VICA Skills Olympics. We went to the Nationals and John coached me and made me rehearse my speech throughout the entire bus ride from Sioux Falls, South Dakota to Cincinnati, Ohio. That was a long bus ride. When we arrived, I knew the speech so well I could not possibly mess it up. Then I went on stage, went blank and forgot where I was in the middle of the speech. I repeated an entire paragraph. I blew it big time, and everyone in the entire auditorium knew it. John simply came over later, smiled, and shook my hand. He told me he was proud because even though I didn't win, he knew I had given my very best. It would have been easy at that point to never walk on stage again, but John told me I had a gift for storytelling, and God would not want me to waste it. He was famous for saying just what he told me that day: "God doesn't make junk!"

Later in life I won a big bid for a huge construction project in Antarctica. My bid narrowly beat the bid John's company placed. After the award, John called me to congratulate me and let me know that the entire industry was counting on me to "not screw this thing up!" I remember that exact quote to this day. Little did my staff know that his urging spread additional emphasis on quality and ensured that this was a project that would become our industry's crown jewel of the South Pole.

I was watching a speaker at a trade association banquet who was extoling the virtues of his products, his services, and his organization. It was truly a picture of narcissism and self-adulation all rolled up into an industry-wide presentation. John and I stood in the back of the room when the speaker finished after taking about 10 minutes longer than allowed. In front of us, two relatively old and grizzled veterans of the industry passed a note back and forth to each other. They were obviously commenting on the merits of the speaker. I mentioned to John that I would love to read that note. Sometime after the luncheon had ended, John approached me and beckoned me over to the table where the note was passed. He grabbed it and slowly unfolded it while we read the three simple words that passed between the men. The note read: "Ego blocks wisdom." John and I reminded each other of that moment for many years to try to keep each other humble.

John came from a small town yet rallied kids, adults, employees to rise up beyond expectations. He himself rose to levels that were unprecedented for a kid from the wrong side of town. He did so against the odds, even becoming the president of a National Trade

Association and leading hundreds of employees. He did so with an eye for service.

John served.

- He served in the U.S. Navy for four years.
- He served at his church, Immaculate Conception.
- He served at the American Legion.
- He served as a coach and teacher of knuckleheads.
- He served as an industry leader at EPSMA and SIPA.
- He served his employees.
- He served by leading a buyout of a major employer in his chosen hometown.
- He served with Lori at both Engaged Encounter and Marriage Encounter.
- He served the Cattlemen's Association.
- He served his marriage, his kids, and his family.

John was a big-thinking visionary and a maverick with a streak of rebellion, but most importantly, he treasured his faith, family, and friends.

John was more than the teacher or the list you find above; he was my friend.

Chapter 8

Belief

Belief in someone cannot be fleeting if it is to have impact. When you believe in someone, it doesn't stop when that person disappoints you or somehow lets you down. When you believe in someone, you go all in, and I mean for the long haul. When someone believes in you, they tend to see you not for who you are now, but who they see you can become. They then invest into that vision. When someone goes all in, you don't just see it, you feel it, and then, after time, you know it. The realization of knowing someone believes in you creates confidence and enhances your abilities while minimizing your doubts.

•••••••••

All In

When deciding how you will treat people, that decision is usually affected, if not dependent, upon how that person comes into your life. My father-in-law, Mel, was a very influential businessman in Duluth, Minnesota, where he served as the general superintendent of the Duluth Missabe and Iron Range Railroad (DM&IR). The general superintendent of a railroad is the de facto chief operating officer. Mel had around 3,200 employees and also served on the board of directors for a sizeable local credit union. He was an elder at Glen Avon Presbyterian Church and was involved in many community organizations where he was generally recognized as a leader in the community and an important cog in the regional economy. He was far above my station in life.

In strolls a 19-year-old welder from South Dakota working in power line and substation construction in Northern Minnesota ready to declare his undying love for Lorraine and Mel's youngest daughter. My future mother-in-law almost had an aneurysm while my soon-to-be father-in-law studied me, asked me questions, and let me know that the task in front of me was pretty sizable. Knowing that, though, he began to mentor me from the second conversation we ever had. He encouraged me and let me know that I was capable. He did not say "You can" marry my daughter, at least not right away. He did say "You can" be a success in life. "You can" go to college! As a matter of fact, he asked where I was going to college, not inquiring if I planned to, but where? I firmly believe that my expressed intention to graduate from college was an unspoken deal breaker as far as getting his blessing to marry Sarah, so off to college I went.

Mel was the exact right person to encourage me along. He was born in Pease, Minnesota in 1925 to the owner of two general stores who also was a farmer. Mel had three siblings with the youngest being 14 years younger than him. He graduated from high school at 16 and was scouted by the Cincinnati Reds baseball team but instead headed to Calvin College in Grand Rapids, Michigan where his studies were cut short. He entered the war effort in the European theater in World War II, but never discussed his experience. The family history indicates that a draft card arrived on his 18th birthday, and he enlisted that very day in the U.S. Army. Apparently, he fought in the Battle of the Bulge, serving under none other than General George Patton. The only thing he ever told me about that war was that it was a "rough go." That generation was sure built of tough fellows.

Mel returned from the war and started college at the University of Minnesota where he graduated on March 18, 1948, with a bachelor's degree in electrical engineering and a bachelor's degree in business administration. He also was a husband and a collegiate athlete. He was married while playing collegiate baseball. Can you imagine playing college sports, taking on a double major, and being married on top of it? He obviously had to put his virtual photographic memory to use those years.

Drafted out of college by the Cincinnati Reds, Mel decided instead to work in a more stable role in engineering. For years, he worked engineering jobs that brought to his family a comfortable life. But Mel was a country kid and still comfortable and grateful to be a country club member.

When Sarah and I got engaged, though, he invited me to join him for dinner at a private dining club in Duluth called the Kitchi Gammi Club. I was a welder during this time and was fortunate to have a collared shirt and single pair of khaki pants. While entering the club, I was informed that jackets and ties were required of "gentlemen." I quickly discovered that they had a room filled with jackets and ties for unexpecting lads like me, and I was offered a jacket and tie so I could stay for dinner. Please understand that this was a high-brow joint I was in, not my traditional local tavern, and I was simply not prepared. Mel immediately put me at ease with his wit and his charm, he accepted me just as I was, and then chuckled because I did not know what escargot were. For the rest of us, they are snails. Yes, people do consume them. As I soon found out, anything is edible with enough butter. Mel got quite a good laugh about my response to eating snails, but he was kind, even though his wife was not as amused with this South Dakota hick.

Mel and Lorraine visited us while in college at the University of South Dakota in Vermillion. He liked to golf and took us out on the local links one summer day. It was unusual for Sarah and me to do anything that was not free in those days, so the golf was a real treat. The good news was that I got to go golfing, the bad news was that it was my first time ever! While I was all over the course, my wife was driving, chipping, and putting me into the ground. I was getting my butt kicked and not enjoying it very much at all. I still don't like golf much or play it very well.

Mel understood my college years because he completed his MBA through the University of Minnesota while working a full-time job. The man could accomplish most anything he set out to do. And while obviously his greatest gift to me was his youngest daughter, Sarah, I also thrived under his belief in me. He convinced me that I could accomplish my goals with the simple words, "You can!"

Thanks, Mel. You told me I could, and I believed you. I hope you are proud!

Chapter 9

Confidence

—————————

Confidence is difficult to quantify because there are so many forms and styles of confidence that can be expressed in various ways. True confidence comes from others and is funneled into you or into something and can be seen in innumerable ways: self-confidence, team confidence, product confidence, or ability confidence. No one comes into the world with true confidence as it is instilled by others and then developed by you. When you earn the confidence others place in you, it is precious and not to be squandered. The price you paid for true confidence is the prepaid tuition you get from meaningful people who have confidence in you. It is crafted and honed based on the life experiences that will either enhance or diminish it. The true confidence gifted to me looks like self-assurance but feels like trust.

· · · · · · · · · ·

Those Who Define

The fourth musketeer of my most influential people born in 1925 is Leroy. He joins my dad, my father-in-law, and Norb as the people who really defined, for me, the greatest generation. I did not meet Leroy until just after college. Sarah and I moved after graduation in Vermillion, South Dakota to the big city. We chose the Minneapolis area because there were no jobs to be had for me locally in March of 1983. So, I finished college before summer began, and we packed up and headed for Plymouth, Minnesota. Our new home was a northwest suburb of the famous Twin Cities of Minneapolis and St. Paul. I really knew no one and did not have a lead on work of any kind. Sarah, with new baby, Ryan, in tow, headed out early, and I arrived with the U-Haul truck the next day. During the lease signing of our new apartment, we heard they needed help cleaning apartments after people moved out, so we jumped right on that. The following Monday morning, with a new suit and tie, I took a stack of 300 resumes and began the process of walking door to door in the local business parks to find a job. I knew the rent would come due soon enough, so there was no time to waste.

About 11 a.m., and after I had heard about 25 people say they weren't interested, I walked into PSM Products, Inc. I knew nothing about them or anything they did. I asked the receptionist for a manager. She asked what I wanted, and I told her I was delivering a resume. She quizzed me a bit and promised that they would give it a look. As I turned to leave, a voice came from behind me and asked how I thought I would get a job going door-to-door like that. I spun around to a tall, distinguished man in a blue suit with a shock of white hair. I replied that before the week was out, someone would be smart enough to hire me. He laughed a big laugh and asked me to step into his office. Leroy wasn't the manager, he was the CEO and founder of this small, but growing, family business. I was immediately drawn to him, and I think he took a shine to me as well. Before I left that office, we negotiated a deal for me to begin work the following morning starting at a whopping $14,500 dollars a year. Hey! That was more than this new graduate was offered to be an assistant manager at K-Mart by 2,500 bucks!

Immediately, I went to the local florist and bought my wife a dozen roses. I delivered them in our new apartment where I was immediately reminded that we could not afford such luxuries. After almost a full minute Sarah turned to me with a shocked expression on her face and exclaimed, "You got a JOB!" Yes, as a matter of fact, I start in the morning! I tried to tell her what they did and how great a gig it would be, but I struggled to explain it from one excited person to another. PSM was a fabricator of flexible materials including foam, rubber, and gasketing materials. We sold custom die-cut materials to manufacturers who put our products in their assembly lines. I had no idea what I would be doing for a living!

I showed up early the next day in my new and only suit and waited for the office to open. Some other folks showed up to work and Tom, who you will read about later in this chapter, let me know I should go home and get on some jeans and a T-shirt as I would be getting dirty. It would be a good bet that I blushed a bit as I said, "Yes, sir," and hustled home to change. After getting comfortable in my jeans, I was shown the warehouse manned by a fellow named, "Sarge." He had an issue with spelling and body odor, but he was the warehouse manager. The place was a total mess of boxes, and Tom told me to help Sarge get organized and get the warehouse squared away. The next week was invaluable as I got to know materials and terminology that Sarge typically had mislabeled. I studied materials, yields, and offal (the part left over after you die cut a piece of foam or sponge rubber). Leroy and Tom had me learning the business from the ground up; it was not the first gift they would give me.

After helping Sarge, I graduated to the production floor for a couple of weeks where I learned the capabilities of the equipment we had in the shop. Here, the business from the production end was far different than the spit and polish the sales team was putting out. What I learned was that this small and growing family-owned business was learning to make parts more efficiently every day. The better I learned the processes, the more value I would bring to the table. Pretty soon I entered the estimating and customer service or inside sales part of my career at PSM. I would put the production floor experiences to use on a daily basis. The better that we laid out or nested the dies that cut the materials, the more money we made, the less scrap we generated, and the happier everyone became. We even began to pull boxes of offal out of the warehouse and use essentially scrap material that was still great for similar parts that could be made from truly prime goods. We all were learning lessons every day.

Leroy invested time in me. He would ask me to lunch with him at least once a week. Many times, his lovely wife, Pearl, would join us, and he would talk about life, careers, and choices, and how they all blended together. His moral compass was always on display, and he was never ashamed to witness his readily evident faith to me by his word and actions. He also instilled lessons in economics from the old school of hard knocks. Because we had another Jim in the office, my new name became "JT." One day, Leroy convinced me that the best price to charge someone was the "highest price that the market could bear." "JT," he said, "the folks who pay the bills look for perfect quality, and they want it on time. They'll always want to pay less, but not if it is wrong or late!" That is one of the life lessons that would serve me immensely throughout my entire career.

One day, after moving the price up to a customer and dramatically increasing both the margins and the order quantity, Leroy stopped all activity in the entire office. He brought everyone in the front office to my desk in a shared office and announced, "Ladies and Gentlemen, I just want you all to know, 'This dog hunts!'" While some may view this as a demeaning comment, it meant the world to me and continues to motivate me even 40 years later.

As I advanced up the ladder at PSM, it became apparent that the sales side of the business had incredible value. Being a firm founded by two exceptional salesmen, it should come as no surprise that my path quickly drifted to the sales side of the house. The Friday afternoon before I was to head out on the road for my first official sales calls, Leroy called me into his office. "JT," he began, "show me one of your business cards." I handed him one of my newly minted sales engineer business cards, and he appeared to read and study it carefully. After he had handed it back, he asked me, "Whose name is on that card?" Thinking he had lost his faculties, I sheepishly but proudly replied that my name was on the card. "No," he said firmly, "my name is on that card, as you are representing me and everyone else in this company when you are carrying that card. So, son, if I ever hear of you stepping out on your wife or drinking too much or even entering a bar alone while on the road, I will fire you! Do you understand me?"

As fast as I could, I replied, "Yes, sir!" or something equally as submissive as I not only feared and respected this man, but I knew he was right. I also knew that he would do exactly what he said. This is one of the greatest favors and life lessons bestowed on me. As I walked out of his office that day, he stopped me and told me another phrase that I still carry in my mind almost daily: "JT, you will do great at this, I know you will!"

Leroy never flaunted or displayed his faith by telling me what to do. He showed us all through the manner he lived his life and how he treated people. Once, before he passed away, I got the chance to return to his office and say hello. The joy on his face when he saw me was incredibly gratifying! That smile was perhaps a larger gift than all the business acumen he taught me. Even though I stopped primarily to say hello, I also wanted him to know that he played a significant role in any success I enjoyed, and I wanted him to know my gratitude to him. Like most everything else, he took the compliment in stride and accepted the praise as a gentleman. I wouldn't have expected anything different.

Just because Leroy told me, "You will!," the confidence he gave me meant, "I did!"

·········

Tom was Leroy's business partner. He also happened to be Leroy's eldest son. This is a relationship model that I was fortunate to use when forming Legacy with my own son some 15 years later. In much the same way that Leroy taught me the "why" to do things, Tom taught me the "how." Tom's lessons were more blunt, more practical, and could be easily employed if you just trusted his system. One thing he convinced me early is that Leroy may have been right when he coached us that the early bird gets the worm, but the proverb needed legs under it. Tom taught me I better be closing deals and getting orders while your competitor still had a toothbrush in his mouth. He taught me to use nights and early mornings to travel from one market to another so that my time on the road was always productive. Tom taught me to plan out my work, which looked almost exactly like this:

- Breakfast early and with a purchasing agent, if possible.
- Be at the client's office at 8:00 AM or earlier, if they are open.
- Start with engineering because they are sharpest in the morning and so are you.
- Ask for an order before noon.
- Take a future customer to lunch.
- Find new customers in the afternoon.
- Purchasing departments have already been disappointed by someone today, be a hero.
- Have advance plans to have dinner with a paying customer to show your appreciation.
- Finish up and drive to the next market while your competitors are sleeping.
- Do your call reports that night, so you don't forget what you promised.
- Repeat.

Tom is the most persuasive individual I have ever encountered. When he said something, you took it to heart because it worked. Add to that the hustle factor and his incredible desire to win and there was no one who could beat him. If you followed in his footsteps, there were few who could keep up with you and even fewer who could match wits with you. Know your product better and your solutions will be better. Solve a problem and you don't win a customer, you build a friendship.

Early growth in this startup made every decision important. I once ordered a huge amount of 3/32" thick material 54 inches wide. The customer mistakenly claimed that they told me to order 60 inches wide. It was a huge mistake and the PSM way meant making a practice of keeping happy customers. It was early enough in my career that I was certain the natural result of "my" error was that I would be fired. In truth, I was sweating bullets because jobs were hard to come by, and it was a huge financial mistake as we were talking about thousands of yards of material that were non-standard. Tom walked into my office, smiled, and said, "JT, you've got a lot of 3/32 grey polyether urethane to sell." Just like that, my solution was to sell this stuff at break even or better. Mercy under pressure from your boss, take note, Jim, learn and remember that lesson well. But the lessons didn't stop there!

Tom once walked me into the John Deere manufacturing plant in Ankeny, Iowa. Immediately, he began asking folks in the engineering office about the biggest problem they had. He didn't really care what their particular problem was, as it likely revolved around sound, liquids, vibration, or efficiency, as with all manufacturing offices. Before long, we were designing a seal for the lid of a new sprayer tank. We left with a commitment for the development of tooling to manufacture a new seal and a proprietary part number.

This product was a simple die cut gasket that would never have huge volume, but it would be very profitable. "Take what you can get, JT," was his lesson that day.

Another time, we went into the factory of the famous recreational vehicle manufacturer Winnebago and strolled into the engineering department like Tom owned the joint. I had never been there, and Tom hadn't been there in years. He asked for an engineer who just happened not to work there anymore. That didn't matter though, Tom just asked who took his place. We got introduced and again Tom challenged the guy to give us a look at his biggest problem. It turns out that their new fuel-efficient RV, the LeSharo, was overheating. He asked the obvious question of why, and the engineer let him know the design couldn't get enough air to the engine. In 10 minutes, Tom had designed a foam hood scoop to be fastened to the underside of the engine hood and had an order for samples and appropriate tooling. The LeSharo lasted for about 10 years, and the overheating issue was forever solved.

When confronted with a problem that could not be solved by an engineering team, Tom made sales because the customer knew he'd get results. One vital client called and needed a gasket that was far larger than our capability. Tom used off-the-shelf materials to design a seal that was about six feet wide and three feet tall. We mitered the corners with a filet knife and welded the corners together with super glue. Then we dipped the corners in a liquid coating like you would find on the handles of pliers. The clients were thrilled with the results, but that meant that we needed a bunch of parts, and we needed them quickly. Tom and another guy drove through the weekend and brought back huge spools of raw materials and we cut, glued, and dipped our way to an early-the-next-week delivery. Nothing could stop him.

Tom is a proud veteran of the United States Army. He was shipped out as a private to Vietnam and served as a non-commissioned officer in the artillery. He ended up as what is commonly referred to as a buck sergeant during the Vietnam War. Today, I thank him for all he taught me and also for serving our nation.

Tom is a hard charging professional whose success led him all across the United States and then to Europe as a problem solver. He put those skillsets to work coaching the rest of his team how to solve problems while looking for opportunities to do what others couldn't or wouldn't. But solving problems was always first.

Tom taught me that you must always, "Ask for the order!" Someone is going to make that product he would insist: "It should always be us." Tom continually reminded me that you must ask for what you want, JT, you must!

Chapter 10

Friendship

A s we are reminded in Proverbs 17:17, a friend loves at all times. A genuine friend is present in your life and connected on a deep level with what is important to you. A friend loves you back, and they do it from every angle. They listen to you and then discern what is in your best interest. They communicate openly about not what you said, but what they heard. There is a mutual trust in friendship that travels beyond the boundaries of ordinary relationships. A friend can be trusted to question and cajole you or have empathy and respect what you are experiencing. They can tell you things others cannot because of their proven investment in you. Friends display love through generous listening and follow up with action.

··········

Justin—Stop and Think

Aside from my brothers and some other family members, the people in my life who I count as friends are frankly very few and far between. The ones who I trust as confidants are far fewer still. At the top of the list is Justin. Our relationship has continued for over 30 years, and if you used common sense only as a yardstick, we should not be close friends. We are very different from one another. Our work paths have been different. For most of those 30 years our area codes, zip codes, and even time zones have been different. Other than hunting, our hobbies don't really match up well either. Justin loves gardening, I think it is lame. Justin loves bee keeping, bees scare me to death. I love airplanes, he doesn't like to fly. I thrive with pressure, he tolerates it, until he doesn't! There is no reasonable supporting evidence that we should be best friends. But we are. Probably because we have done many seasons of life together, and that included some really hard stuff.

When I first began to understand that a relationship with Jesus had nothing to do with religion in the classic sense, I knew no men who believed as I did. My first exposure was through a guy by the name of Kevin who hunted geese and worked at the same place where Sarah waited tables. Kevin started the discussion and then set me up to meet Justin. I reluctantly went to a church that was located within the auditorium of a public school. When that first service finished, I jetted for the door. My thoughts were clear: one and done! Just before my escape and right on the precipice of my exit, this dude steps in front of me and said, "I hear you hunt?" This was super weird for me, but I responded, "Yes, I do." He replied, "Great, you're having lunch at my house, our wives are already talking." I was almost in shock when I turned around and Sarah had been waylaid by a lady who happened to be Justin's wife. The good news was that we had elk burgers for lunch and the rest, as they say, is history.

Justin showed me how to spend time reading the Bible every day. He didn't do it by guilting me or preaching to me about my need for it. He did it by getting his butt out of bed early and actually doing it. Then he spoke often and softly about what he learned that morning. He told stories of how God's Word impacted him. He modeled a relationship that made me want to have that kind of relationship—and not just with a book, but with the Creator of the universe. Justin is the reason that I started to get up every day at 4:54 a.m. I did that for about 30 years so I could get some time with God before being the first one at work.

As it turns out, Justin and I are the same age. Sarah and Cheryl are the same age. We got married in the same year. They ended up with five kids, we ended up with five kids. Our eldest were the same age, and we each have more grandkids than most anyone we know. Jim and Sarah with 14 and Justin and Cheryl with 20—and counting. We both adopted children into our families with the same conviction. (These are our children, for better or worse, we pick them and give them over to Jesus.) There has never been a difference in the steadfast love between our biological kids and our chosen kids. We have shared our parenting joys, struggles, victories, defeat—and virtually everything in between. This is one of the things that unites us indelibly and irrevocably.

Hard times usually craft strong relationships. Justin once called me when I was acting like a jerk to my wife. I didn't feel like listening to a lecture at that moment, so when he called me on the phone in my truck, I didn't pick up. He called again and I hit ignore. He called a third time but this time I picked up with a curt, "What do you need?" Justin simply responded with a comment no one else could have gotten away with, "I hear you're being stupid," he said. Normally that might be a good means of getting hit in the mouth, but I knew that he was right, and he began to deescalate me because he knew me well. I can always count on Justin to give me the truth no matter how ugly it is. This was his way of saying that I needed to stop and think.

Justin and I both had a couple careers where we were high achievers. Justin ran a manufacturing line that produced lift trucks used by linemen and even my tower guys. He went from an hourly assembly line guy to being in charge of an entire product line. During that same time, he finished his bachelor's degree and was the first in his family ever to do so. After 25 years, that manufacturing company went out of business after an ill-advised ESOP or Employee Stock Option Program or employee-based buyout. After that, Justin went to work at a production supply house where he managed multiple locations servicing commercial and construction accounts as a manager. He spent another 20 years in that second career and has been a great blessing to his employers and the employees who worked for him. During that time, he also ran the longest paper route in Denver and paid off his mortgage! The guy is an amazing work horse.

Justin is a big game hunter. He is a man who, like me, does not apologize for the ethical harvesting of wild game animals. I'm better at bird hunting, and he is the ultimate big game meat hunter. His family, to my knowledge, has seldom purchased any meat, with the exception of bacon, from the store.

When he hunts, the man goes all in all the time. Once, my son, Ryan, Justin, and I, were on an unguided caribou hunt in Alaska. It was an incredible experience and very primitive. Justin saw a nice bull walking around the base of a mountain we were approaching. Everyone who has ever hunted caribou on the tundra knows you cannot catch them if you are seeing their backside. You just can't. But Justin quipped, "I'll be right back!" He then disappeared running up and over the mountain. He wanted to take the short cut over the top as the big bull walked around the base. I told Ryan he would never catch the bull because Justin was climbing up and across slide shale. I was preparing to go fetch a broken Justin when we heard a rifle shot from a long way off! Justin, literally ran down a caribou on its home turf. Talk about stop and think!

Not many people get to see the softer side of my buddy, but there is photographic evidence herein to prove that he has one. We spent our 35th anniversary in Hawaii on Kauai with Justin and Cheryl. This time was one of the best vacations I have ever had (without a gun). Four people who just wanted to hang out and celebrate the duration of their love for their spouse and their deep and abiding friendship with one another. These are the depths of friendship that are forged in the difficulties and victories of life and then stand the test of time because they always serve the other first and God before that.

Our joint 40th anniversary was to be spent on a cruise north but when Covid stepped in, we pushed the celebration out to our 43rd anniversary. We shared the big 43 in the 49th state on an Alaskan cruise.

Almost every time I get ready to lose my temper, Justin encourages me to just stop and think. He's not going to preach or lecture to me. He doesn't psychoanalyze stuff or ask me what my motives are, he sees or hears that I am angry and just listens. He's not trying to score points or win me over by being right. Most all the time, he just listens and then responds and tries to lead me down a path where I can just stop and think!

Chapter 11

Influence

W hat is a pastor? According to Wikipedia and Google, America's apparent new source of truth, a pastor is someone who is "… the leader of a Christian congregation who also gives advice and counsel to people from the community or congregation." While this definition contains truth, I find it to be more than a bit shallow and lacking full understanding. Just like a CEO or other senior leader, a pastor, to me, is defined by who they are in real life and proved out by what gets modeled to those who are in their sphere of influence. Only a few pastors have had a profound effect on my life over the past 30 or so years since I became a follower of Jesus. Some of the pastors had a negative effect—we won't waste any ink on that—but others have been illustrations of men whose examples have created such a profound impact that they significantly changed my life for the better. How they did that may be surprising.

· · · · · · · · ·

The Pastors

<u>Pastor Ed:</u> Ed was the first fellow I ever met who was totally comfortable teaching about the Bible from the actual Bible. His biblical literacy was off the charts, and he insisted that the book was a personal letter to me and written entirely without error. As mentioned, I'm not the best student on the planet so, naturally, I asked him to prove it. Ed's demeanor was always gentle, and his delivery had a different level of kindness that felt foreign to me. I was a construction guy and very new to all this Jesus stuff. His conviction drew me in, and his patience and compassion held me there while I learned so much in a very short time. The thing I took away from Pastor Ed is that he was deeply in love with Jesus. His effect on me was deep, lasting, and profound.

Ed was also the man who instilled in me the knowledge that the scriptures could and should be used for the counseling of those who are having difficulties. Ed was one of the early pioneers of the Biblical Counseling movement across the USA. He resurrected what has become the International Association of Biblical Counselors. With his example, I decided I, too, would like to get certified for counseling, and as such, I wanted desperately to absorb and know the material. I was required to write an abstract on the book, *Why Christians Can't Trust Psychology* by Dr. Ed Bulkley. I had read the book previously and devoured it again. This time I took notes and looked for things where the author (Ed) could have improved or even missed the mark. My review was thorough and perhaps even brutal. I sent it in with the first package of abstracts and found out after it was shipped who my mentor would be, Dr. Ed Bulkley, aaarrrggghhhhh! Ed handled it with such grace and openness that I was stunned. He wrote comments like he hadn't considered my remarks prior and "Good Perspective!" Had I known that the author was going to be reading—much less grading my work—I probably would have been more measured in my analysis. Instead, with my raw analysis resting between us, I was shown mercy and grace by someone who I greatly respected and admired. This lesson in gentleness, humility, and kindness from God, through Pastor Ed, has never left me.

He was my first pastor in my new walk with Jesus, and I will be forever indebted to him for showing me what it looked like when you love Jesus: Go *all in* on your conviction and faith!

<u>Richard:</u> Pastor Richard, who earned a doctorate, was like Pastor Ed in that he was a gifted leader and preacher. Pastor Richard affected me in the area of work more than anywhere else. Initially, he showed me that if you work hard at being a shepherd, it is hard work. He was the guy who was up and in the office every day at zero dark 30. Like me, he was usually at work before most everyone else. His staff generally had difficulty keeping up with him. Even the young folks were amazed at both his pace and his endurance. Doc was not a sprinter, but never quit the marathon that was so difficult for non-type A people to understand. He showed me that what he did—caring for people—was hard work, but it wasn't something I had seen previously from a clergy member. Maybe it was there to see, but I personally hadn't noticed. In many ways, our personalities were in sync, so we were a good match—and perhaps sometimes an irritant in both directions.

Much like his work ethic at the church he founded, Pastor Richard worked hard at praying for people. And he did so early and often. He would spend the first hours of his day on a hidden kneeler behind a bookcase in his office as though he were praying in a closet, out of the public eye, much the way we are instructed to pray in Matthew 6. He often spoke of his prayer life, although never in a boasting manner. It was so important to him, in fact, that he created and taught a process or plan for keeping your prayer life a priority. He taught me and so many others to pray using a system that would encourage both discipline and authenticity. He showed me that God hears every prayer but responds when it is best—not on my time frame and not my will, because I am not God.

To this day I am compelled to pray each morning for a list of people in a systematic way because of the example set for me by Doc.

<u>Bob:</u> Some might argue that Bob couldn't have had that much impact on my life simply because I never met him. His influence, though, has been mighty. Over the years, I spent a great deal of time with him on the internet. When the internet was freshly minted, I needed some guidance and found it in a daily devotional called, *Day by Day Grace*. It was like he personally spoke to me every morning via the Blue Letter Bible. God revealed to me through Bob that I had been fully forgiven. I spent virtually every weekday with his writing.

In 2012, I decided to pursue a certification in biblical counseling. The second book I was to read and complete an abstract on was, *How To Counsel God's Way*, by Bob Hoekstra. It was like spending time with an old friend. His work moved me so much that I decided to contact him to let him know his decades-long impact on me. By the time I made that decision, though, I was too late. Bob went home to Jesus in 2011.

<u>Pastor Jack:</u> Recently, I met another pastor whose impact on me has been profound. So grateful am I for Jack that when Sarah and I would vacation in Palm Springs, California, we would schedule times and places where it would be easy to drive the 75 miles and attend Calvary Chapel Chino Hills. We would do so based upon this guy who was changing the face of American Christianity to one of bold and intentional following of Jesus. Pastor Jack challenges us to act like Jesus by doing what he modeled for us and wrote for us in the Bible. The ministry of Calvary Chapel and Pastor Jack were the first to reveal to me that I have a duty to engage the culture, not just a church. Yes, I had done stuff through local efforts and even helped with bigger national ministry things, but intentional, rather than incidental engagement was mandated. Pastor Jack let me know that it was expected because of my love for the One who saved me. Pastor Jack let me know that if I didn't engage, someone else would, and they may not have the same motives. Engagement should also be a thankful response to forgiveness, not some sort of a method to earn mercy. Efforts should include engaging my family, my work, my church, my community, and even my country. In a very short time, in my opinion, Pastor Jack has become America's pastor. This is a role that was previously held by giants like D. L. Moody, Billy Graham, and John MacArthur. Pastor Jack continually reminds us all, through multiple formats, electronic and in person, to engage because Jesus is returning soon!

<u>David:</u> Pastor David is the pastor at Calvary Chapel Star. It is my home church where Sarah and I have attended since the very first Sunday it opened. We had been praying for a Bible preaching church for quite a while and started a search for a local church in earnest about the time that the announcement for Calvary Chapel Star launched. This was a hopeful sign to Sarah and me because Pastor David spent over 20 years at Calvary Chapel Chino Hills under the mentorship of, you guessed it, Pastor Jack.

Early during the introduction to Pastor David, I concluded that he was not trying to be Jack. He was his own man and had a grasp of the scriptures that was inverse to his chronological age. He is also a gifted communicator and a very coachable man. In my estimation, he is a modern version of Timothy, who studied under Paul. Pastor David is a hardworking man with a supportive family and a vision for touching his part of the world for Jesus. Normally, I would resist being led by a younger man. It is not their fault, it is just how I am built. Pastor David is an exception to the rule. At around 40 years old, he is well-versed and balanced and has won me over time and again while helping me to deepen my faith by his example. He once told me, "Do more, time is short!" I will follow him as he follows Christ—and do so proudly! Pastor David is also in awe of what the Savior has done. He has shown me to relax and gather in, with awe, just how incredible God is.

What do these five men have in common? Like any good type A person, I made a list:

- They take seriously and are faithful to their calling as a shepherd and pastor.
- They work hard.

- They personally inspired me to do better.
- They all have big visions of what could be—they look farther ahead.
- They communicate well.
- They largely defer credit to God, always keeping their egos in check.
- They focus on the local church and put other ministries second.
- They married well, all blessed with supportive wives.

I will be the first to admit that it may be strange to put this much emphasis on spiritual things in a largely secular book, but these guys were chosen by God to help build me. The Lord gets any credit, but these fellows responded to try and sharpen me for Christ. They have each impacted my life in their own way and on a significant level. If you don't yet have a relationship with Jesus and want to know more, get ahold of me, I would love to just chat about my story and yours. Any of them would also welcome your call!

Chapter 12

Intensity

ntensity is a character trait that provides drive, motivation, and focus. When appropriately channeled, it can bring forth results that are extraordinary. And, while it can manifest itself as a quiet power force, a calm fixed sense of purpose, or a white-hot fire in the belly, you'll know when you see it. Appropriate intensity crafts a desire to move ever forward with a vision for the destination. It lifts people to focus and outperform their known capabilities especially when shared within a team environment. But the sword of intensity has two edges, and they are both sharp. Wield this tool of advantage carefully and thoughtfully.

· · · · · · · · · ·

My Premier Era

It's fair to confess that I have probably learned more from failures than I have any successes. Those hard lessons get etched pretty deeply into your brain. So, having the Denver construction market die back in the early 90s, I found myself needing to lead Sarah through another near-bankruptcy experience. Or, maybe she led me? One day, when things were looking about as grim as they could be, Sarah came down into my basement office and said she thought I should call this fellow in Seattle who had multiple times offered me a career path. Being desperate and trying not to show it, I let her know I would call him but with the caveat that I would, "NOT EVER move to either California or Seattle!"

Two weeks later, I arrived at my new job in Kent, Washington, a suburb of Seattle, on April Fool's Day, 1993. I am certain that every experience, both victory and defeat, helped prepare me for the tasks I needed to execute to turn around the biggest loser division of Premier Industries. What I did not yet realize were the corporate politics that lay ahead and would provide roadblocks to our success as a business unit, although those lessons were to be learned soon enough.

What was Premier Industries? Like every business, it was a collection of people. Five of those people had such a significant impact on me that they are mentioned here. I will only speak of the positive things as I am blessed with a memory that forgets most of the nasty stuff that takes place when making sausage. The five are not listed in order of importance as I see them as all equally important. They are listed in the order that I met them. The first two were born in England and impressed upon me the love they had for the USA and how their chosen home was factually, "The last bastion for capitalism in the world."

Mike: From 1986 through 2002, Mike was the voice of reason at Premier. He served as the vice president of the Construction Products Division for 16 years. Mike was the reason I landed there in the first place. He recruited me from the very day I met him and was always pleasantly persistent. When I finally placed the call to Premier, he was the one I called. I had reached him in California where he was solving both sales and production problems and living near the beach in Santa Monica. He told me that he was thrilled to get my call, and he would have the CEO return my call ASAP!

Mike taught me much about delegation. Because I knew the product and the manufacturing process better than he, he just cut me loose. Some of the gems he taught me came only from the wisdom of an experienced mentor. Mike told me right after I was hired, "If I have to do your job, I don't really need you." He taught me in the corporate environment that, "the numbers never lie, because if the numbers lie we're all screwed!" Most of all, Mike knew that I was intense and driven, so he gave me free reign to learn, even if it meant making mistakes along the way.

He encouraged me to get the top line up and then craft solutions for tweaking the bottom line. "You cannot have profit without any volume, Jimmy!" he would say. He was one of the first who instilled in me the notion that you can never "scrimp your wallet to prosperity." He also taught me to be balanced in presenting opportunities, because everything looks good at a distance. He mentored me in the world of growth through acquisitions as we made two significant acquisitions of companies in my division. We also added a new location from growth that was generated through sheer audacious salesmanship!

Mike had an intensity of his own. While he was educated in England as an architect, he had done many things. There is no doubt that he did them all with jovial energy and his positive vigor. I am reminded of this from a trip to Japan I led where Mike was in a following role as I spoke the language a bit and could at least get around. Upon arrival in Japan, he decided it was time to get something to eat. I obliged and led him out of the hotel. Soon after, he just took a right hand turn down a dark and kind of scary looking street. I cautioned, and he replied, "You only live once, Jimmy!" He ultimately found a local patron's-only food joint. Mike wanted to truly have the local experience. They served fish and rice, which was no problem, except that the fish were swimming in a tank, and they wanted to know which meal we wanted. I was balancing life between the brash Englishman and the proprietor who did not enjoy our company. With a wave of his hand, Mike just said, "Give me what he's having," and pointed to the food on the table next to us. I shyly agreed and asked for rice and cooked fish. They delivered a dish to me with a couple small green fish on rice that looked like whole grilled minnows. Mike got a scoop of ice with three whole shrimp on it. The shrimp were grey. We sat a moment, looked at each other wondering what to do when Mike asked, "How do we eat them?" "I don't know," I replied. He beckoned the waitress over and attempted to ask her. All of the sudden, one of the shrimp jumped almost clear off the plate. I leapt up and almost tipped over the table, my big American knee catching the edge. It was quite a scene. Mike simply pulled the head off, sucked the brain out and ate the tail in record time. "Freshest shrimp I've ever had!" he bellowed. The entire joint erupted in laughter, and I enjoyed my minnows and rice.

Mike taught me about relationships and tagged me with an urgency label that stuck. When I got in hot water over quick decisions that were based on gut feel and my knowledge of the industry, he had my back. He often told our C-Suite team that, "Jim has a 'bias for action,' leave him alone and thank God that he's on our side!" Mike had many opportunities to submarine me in a corporate environment as I had a knack for knocking corporate bureaucrats out of the way. But Mike valued the results. He taught me to do so as well.

· · · · · · · · ·

Mick: Mick is the man who could push my buttons better than anyone on the planet! Mike, above, was the envoy, peace maker, and interpreter between Mick and me. He once told me that Mick and I were so much alike that we would never get along. While he may have been right, Mick had enough foresight and experience to know just the right thing to say and just the right time to say it. He could get me to generate results like no other boss I would ever have. He would poke and prod using ego, pride, testosterone, and my own competitive nature to "help" me along. Mick was truly the product of a poor English cobbler who came from nothing to be a multimillionaire by his intensity and sheer force of his will.

He taught me that endless possibilities were waiting, as long as you had a better plan than the other guy. When many people would think in ones, managers would think in tens. Mick was already thinking about thousands. He was a visionary and made me want to emulate him in business. His work ethic was embedded into every part of his life. I never met someone who worked harder at everything than Mick. His cars were cleaner, his desk was clearer, his shoes held a brighter polish, and he performed every task himself. I was blessed to be a part of this inner circle for seven years. This team turned around a company and its culture, and took a business from 25 million in revenue in 1986 to over 1,000 employees and over 200 million in 1999. What a ride! The incentive pay system that

Mick set up for his senior team also funded the startup that became Legacy Telecommunications, Inc. His intensity was contagious. and I was happy to take his example into my next adventure.

·········

Paul: My first week at Premier had me dealing with a fellow team member who was our supplier of expanded polystyrene. The foam product had to be aged enough and cut perfectly flat and square to suit my fledgling manufacturing plant. John, my production manager, came to me enraged and complained that our sister company kept sending us second-rate product. After about the third call to Paul to get it corrected, I threw a block of his foam on the roof of my Chevy Blazer and drove the half mile to his plant. I unstrapped the four-by-eight foot block of foam that was almost six inches thick and wrestled it through the door and front office and unceremoniously threw it across Paul's desk. If I remember correctly, Paul smirked, said he would get right on it, and kind of dismissed me. Before I even got back to my office, Mike called and let me know that Paul thought I was going to work out at Premier just fine. Paul had let Mike know that we finally had someone in the "Loser" structural products division who cared. Further, Paul let Mike know that I knew what I was talking about and had busted him for it. They had a great laugh together while I was fuming mad.

Paul's calm demeanor was almost the polar opposite of my growing intensity. He slowly and methodically introduced me to the concept that work wasn't as important as I had made it, but his incremental and repeated prodding finally came to a head one day. I asked him, with emphasis, just what it was that he thought I was doing wrong. Paul simply said, "Jim, I love my wife." I was more than a bit offended and responded that I did, too. We were both followers of Jesus and knew where our priorities should be. Paul gently scolded me that my work at Premier was too important to me and too much of my attention was being gobbled up by a machine that would never appreciate me or love me as much as my family did.

His impact on me can never be minimized. It is one of the things that caused me to reevaluate how important my job—and the stuff— were to me. It may have led to one of the moments that would later have me walk away from an incredible job and career where I was being rewarded so handsomely. Paul never truly got an appropriate thank you for that day and his impact on my life for just letting me know how much he cared for his beloved wife, Kippy. I owe him one!

· · · · · · · · ·

My Operations Guys: The next two fellows worked directly under me for quite a few years. They would probably say that I was a hard-nosed manager and only focused on winning. The truth is, they were the ones doing the winning and even managed to bring in a ton of business from the Pacific Rim as we became a significant exporter. Our employee base, revenue, and bottom line exceeded everyone's expectations, except us three. We turned the business from a loser to a winner in nine months. We grew the division sevenfold in seven years with over 15% EBITDA or earnings almost every single year. We also scaled it to be a repeatable enterprise and an attractive target for acquisition by both private equity and strategic investors.

· · · · · · · · ·

Steve: Steve is one of the best salesmen I have ever met. He never had a superior skill set or the stature that would immediately draw someone to trust him, but his ability to solve problems coupled with an overwhelming desire not to lose kept his motor running at high RPMs every day. I don't even know if he loved to win so much as he hated losing. We never enjoyed the win celebrations for very long because Steve was on to the next deal. He started out as a salesman for me at Premier, then became sales manager, and ultimately my replacement. His intensity matched his ice blue eyes, and we chose to get along because we needed one another. Any success I enjoyed at Premier was largely due to the efforts of others, and he is chief among them.

Steve got the short end of the stick when I left Premier, probably in large part because he wasn't me. The folks who originally hired him could never get past the fact that he remained a "fresh-from-college" kid in their eyes. In truth, he became a better manager of people, processes, and product than I had ever been. Fortunately, that was recognized by another firm, and his success in business and life are now legendary. He went from managing a small manufacturing plant to growing one of the largest insulation distribution and service businesses in the USA. I am so thankful Steve was who he was and where he was during the time where every moment and every contract meant our joint survival.

••••••••

Greg: Known by a few of us as Hannibal, Greg is an intensely fierce competitor. Soon after starting at Premier, I found out that the fellow everyone missed was Greg. Greg did this…Greg knows that…Do it like Greg showed you! Every time I turned around someone would say that name. I finally got the time or at least the wisdom to call this Greg fellow and invite him to lunch so I could meet him. He had been forced out by the previous manager, and it was because the other guy was insecure and felt threatened when other people were succeeding. What I found in Greg was a young man who had the most superior product knowledge, process knowledge, and tribal knowledge of anyone who worked there. He could get along with our production team. He led the engineering and drafting efforts, he was in charge of customer service and knew all the weaknesses of the sales team and how to motivate them to improve. By the end of our lunch, I had offered him a job, but he would not accept. He didn't want to return to the toxic culture from before and wasn't convinced that I was the right guy to turn it around. Fortunately for me, Greg did some homework and accepted the job after about a week of keeping me on pins and needles.

Greg was one of the solutions to crafting a new culture. He managed me from a subordinate role and protected me from things I couldn't see coming. My plate was full as we were in a full turnaround mode while adding extreme organic growth, new people, facilities, equipment, and acquisitions. Greg handled an amazing amount of stuff that most would see as tedious but was incredibly important to the success of the enterprise being scaled on a go-forward basis. He had an incredible work ethic and never once complained. Greg became a location manager and started up our greenfield operation in Phoenix, Arizona. He moved on to become an incredibly successful technical expert in project, process, and engineering management both in the U.S. and abroad.

With both Greg and Steve, who were always playing tricks on me, the time came for a lesson. We stood near the top of a double black diamond run at Heavenly, the famous ski resort at Tahoe. As I closed in on the edge, I let my ski tips lean out over the fiercely intimidating run. The guys joined me just off my right side. This was truly a peacocking moment. We were all more than a bit put back by the view looking down. With recent fresh powder, it would be easier, but this hill was still a monster. "Well, gents, I think the time has come to just commit," I said. I looked over at two young aggressive guys who wanted to beat me down the hill and beat me badly. "Are you ready?" I queried; they responded, "Yes." I stuck my poles into the ground and let out a full-on attack scream and jumped. While I jumped up, they jumped out. They went hurdling down the slope, and I turned toward the green cat track to have a nice gentle run to the more moderate blue and an enjoyable trip down the mountain. We met at the bottom, and I was fresh and happy, they in turn were exhausted and had eaten some snow, it looked like more than once! They asked why in the world I did that. I replied with a quote from Ronald Reagan, "Gents," I said, "you've got to trust, but verify." Practical jokes sometimes earn a payback!

I am so proud to have had Steve and Greg work with me for those seven years. They gave me a large floor standing globe when I left Premier. They let me know that I gave them the world and they were just trying to return the favor. They gave me confidence that was born from their loyalty, allegiance, their friendship, and, of course, their intensity. Premier shaped me for the future, but the people of Premier helped shape me for a life that would get bigger and more meaningful than just work!

Chapter 13

Trust

=====

ntegrity is a word that is dramatically overused today because it is not understood. I often see advertisements for service firms that promise integrity but are simply chasing money. The reason they use integrity as an advertising slogan is that somehow it lends emotional credibility to their ploy or their profession. Integrity is so deeply personal that it cannot be used to draw comparisons. You could never say you have more integrity than the other guy, because you could never measure his. What does become evident over time is the fruit of integrity. Integrity is choosing to do the right thing even when it is costly, difficult, and when no one will know. Integrity is the tree that bears much fruit over time and gets noticed on a reputational basis. Integrity cannot be quantifiably measured, but it can be seen. But it can only be seen through calendars, not clocks. The time-tested fruit of integrity has always yielded trust!

•••••••••

Most people know me through my association with Legacy. I did that longer and with more success than any other venture. None of that would have been possible without my partner, Ryan Tracy. I don't mean a marriage partner like my wife. I don't mean a relative partner like my brothers, sister, or other family. I don't mean a family partner like the other children or grandkids. I mean a business partner who literally grew up alongside me sharing all the risks, responsibilities, fears, and rewards of boot strapping a startup. This is the business we nurtured through thick and thin including multiple transactions with private equity entities. Ryan Tracy is that partner. He also is my son, my confidant, my fellow tradesman, and an engaging entrepreneur. He has gone from being coached to coaching. Like my wife, he keeps me grounded with truth without regard for my thin skin. Like Justin, he is my hunting partner and life-long best friend. Like my other kids, he is kind to me when I need it, honest when I do as well. Ryan knows my thoughts because we learned how to think out loud with one another in an office of 470 square feet. We built families, homes, towers, memories, and a business feeding hundreds of families without borrowing money from a bank. We raced to the mailbox to look for checks that may have come in the mail and celebrated together when the checks were there. We missed payroll for ourselves, but no employees ever did. We funded paychecks for our employees from our own savings accounts. We did all of this, by God's grace and with amazing women by our side. We invested in people, businesses, and real estate together. We counted wins, losses, joys, and trials. We had people we genuinely trusted treat us badly, and we kept moving. These experiences together make Ryan much more than a partner. But, yes, he is my partner!

After leaving my former position with Premier, I did a turn-around of a National Trade Association for a little over a year. We moved it from Washington, D.C. and from expensive architect lobbyists to me, a grow or die capitalist. After a year, it was a successful and bluntly a boring business to be in. Further, I was tired of and no longer wanted to play the game of Board politics. I was on the lookout for something different.

At the same time, in early 1999, Ryan started working at a local tower construction company doing some of the same work I had done around his age. I went out to his site and was concerned with the lack of leadership as a 19 and 17-year-old were running a new tower building project. The two of them had very little experience, supervision, or training and only a slight knowledge of safety. I was able to help them out when they got into snags on the site but began to see the opportunity in what appeared to be a ready to boom communication tower construction industry. One night at our dinner table, I let Ryan know that I thought he should quit his job. I didn't really think it was safe and was worried he would get hurt or even killed there. He let me know that he liked his job, he liked the money, and if I thought I would be so good at it, we should do it on our own. He was truly the one to propose starting Legacy Telecommunications.

Ryan has, over three decades, put on display a fierce sense of loyalty that is coupled with an eye for what is fair. It is such a part of who he is that our family has put a name on it. We call it the "Fairness Doctrine." If in Ryan's mind something is not fair, and that means for the little guy or underdog in the equation, it is NOT

FAIR! Not only is he usually right in these discussions or decisions, it is virtually impossible to change his mind. He has taught me to think more about the people in the process and less about the outcome. He has taught me to try and put people and their emotions higher on my priority list while still keeping the bigger picture in focus. I am very simple; some would say entirely black and white. All good or all bad, end of story. Ryan occupies way more middle ground as long as you do not offend the fairness doctrine. He has a terrific grasp of the shades of grey. One time, he stepped into my office, closed the door, and sat down. Anyone paying attention could tell that he had something serious to talk about. In typical Ryan fashion, he started with asking how I was doing and showed his penchant for caring about the individual more than the topic at hand. After confirming that he had understood there was no immediate pressing need distracting me and that I was okay, he continued. "Jim," he said, "I was just wondering if anyone told you that you are really bad at taking the temperature in the room?" I do not even remember what the issue was because Ryan was helping me focus on an area that I needed to improve in. He explained that a person should not just walk into a room and consider that they have the accurate point of view, the correct answer, and obviously the best response. He was not only fair with his assessment of me, but he was also right. Ry is one of the few over the years with enough backbone to bring a personal issue up. We have continually challenged one another in that fashion since he was 10 years old. He was the kid who needed to fully understand "the why" and then it had to clear the fairness doctrine.

Ryan was homeschooled for most of his years, so his mom gets all the credit. I was on the road far too much, and Sarah raised a young man who had no difficulty asking questions. When I was gone, he also understood that he was the man of the house. He learned to make decisions and to work hard, really hard. This led him to enjoy the money he made, and he went from scooping the neighbor's dog poop to mowing the lawns. He bought his own lawn mower and figured out he could make more with a chainsaw. He purchased a new chainsaw and discovered he could sell the wood he cleared for the neighborhoods after a storm. This led him to purchase his own truck with dollars that were the result of hard work. He bought a truck with his own cash at 16 years old. Those lessons taught him the value of a dollar and the effort it took to get one.

Perhaps the greatest offering Ryan gave to me was his confidence. I knew stacking steel and business. He knew the technical side of the telecommunications business and how to execute. Our first outside employee was quite a bit older than Ryan but was led quite ably by a kid who just turned 18. Our second employee had to be taught a lot of the ropes as far as wireless was concerned and was older than me. Ryan led this first crew through the grind of not having enough of anything. But he did so and then we grew out of our facilities to the point of continually bursting at the seams. He still does that kind of thing today. He is a serial entrepreneur and a risk taker who has thick skin and a heart of gold. I am the partner who likes the easier path that is more comfortable. Ryan just wants it done right and on time.

Almost everyone gets a story in this book. I have so many about our years working together but the ones that come to mind always have a bit of sarcasm attached to them. Ryan was delivering a mountain top generator to a remote site in Montana with a long line helicopter lift for the delivery. This secluded site was far into the National Forest and had significant travel restrictions. Even so, he brought the customer with him who became quite excited at the whoop, whoop sound of the rotors of the incoming chopper. The client was quite a bit older than anyone on site and began to stress out while talking a lot about the incoming aerial load. He asked if Ryan had ever done this kind of thing before? With a typical smirk, Ryan quipped right back to the purchaser, "No we've never done this before, but I watched a YouTube video on it last night."

Ryan and his wife, Heidi, have raised four boys born in a tad over four years. These young men mean a great deal to me as my eldest four grandsons. They have turned into stand-up guys, all taller than me, who reflect a raised-in-the-country manhood. The most common phrase around their ranch for many years was: "That looks like it's going to hurt." When the boys persisted and tried it anyway, they usually found out that their dad was correct! My guess is that he is still building men.

Finally, Ryan has been a model and trained up literally hundreds of young men in our business. He fashioned thinking leaders who in turn used his example to duplicate what he had done. They are now in positions of leadership of crews, departments, divisions, and businesses. His example helped build all the people who worked for him, worked with him, and me, his partner.

Ryan, thanks for being you, I couldn't have done it without you, and I wouldn't have wanted to!

Chapter 14

Leadership

The Legacy Era

When building a business, one of the most difficult things to assess is someone's ability to lead a group of people. Every business must have a leader. But when starting out, how do you know who is right for the job—especially as the company begins to grow, prosper, and extend into multiple categories and time zones? It's taken decades, but I've come to learn that there are a set of characteristics that manifest themselves in virtually every great leader I have known. Without one of these three characteristics, your company will be lacking. Consider these three: humility, heart, and hustle.

If someone has these traits, I believe they can be trained to become the leader of any team or organization. The reason I say trained is that leaders are formed and forged by something other than what can be taught on an academic level. I maintain it cannot be taught, in the purely academic sense, because in my experience, leadership must be modeled. Looking back over three decades of leadership, the advantage of hindsight is remarkable. The best leaders, I have seen, are those who have allowed me to observe their good work. Most of the time they were not teaching, they were simply doing the things that needed doing. In medicine, for example, there is a proven model of teaching. The model begins with the process of watching a procedure. Then, quickly, the watcher performs (under supervision) one of the procedures recently watched. The watcher then teaches the procedure to someone else.

This technique has benefited innumerable leaders in my sphere of influence over the decades. I've so enjoyed seeing team members who watched me lead become leaders in their own right. Then, as time has passed and opportunities have presented themselves, the benefit came back to me. I learned from them as they modeled the attributes of leadership through a new generation of challenges. Indeed, the students have become the teachers of leadership.

• • • • • • • • •

Why is humility one of the three most crucial traits? Because humility defers to the needs of the people who are carrying out the mission. Humility doesn't care who gets the credit and always shields the team by accepting blame. There was never a more unlikely leader in my mind than JM. He entered our offices just out of high school, and we hired him simply to keep his mom happy. She was our office manager at the time, and we could not afford to lose her. JM came in as a video game aficionado but also had a latent or perhaps undiscovered gift for computer software integration and how it would relate to communications network interfaces. He quickly developed an appetite to know how and why stuff worked. While under the tutelage of Ryan Tracy, he became a lead in our tower troubleshooting division. His quick study and a new ambition to please the customer and get ahead, launched him from gamer nerd to tower rock star. But you'd never spot arrogance in his assent. Ryan and JM moved to Eastern Washington where, together, they launched a greenfield or startup division in the small town of Ritzville. JM has worked to grow that location into the largest private employer in the town. Further, he has become a Legacy legend as a guy who rose from the field to be the Vice President of Operations. JM is walking talking evidence that first impressions can be unreliable. JM continues to beat the odds by putting the team's needs in front. He is often the quiet coach at the back of the room who is silently cheering for his team who is winning.

· · · · · · · · ·

Heart is trickier to explain as it cannot be adequately defined as an attribute of leadership. Unlike humility or hustle there is no definition or performance measurement of heart. I consider it one of the vital three traits because while I am unable to define it, I know it when I see it. There are so many occasions where the use of heart appears as a verb or action, rather than simply a feeling. Tyson Irish has demonstrated *heart* over the years in so many ways. Once, he left our company, as some do, because of a need to relocate or simply because he thought the grass looked greener somewhere else. Like a boomerang, though, Tyson found he wanted to return to our company. He went away from us on multiple occasions only to return with a fuller understanding of life, work, and the benefit of new experiences he gained while away. At our company, we have always encouraged people to do what they were meant to do while improving their situation in life. People who stay and are not content with where they are bring that to work with them every day. We believe those people are better off going elsewhere to figure out whatever is creating those contentment issues. But it takes real heart first to see the need to make a change and then to return when you have gathered the life experiences you may learned along the way. Like many people, Tyson is afraid of heights so his work as a tower worker was a daily struggle. He had an opportunity to take a job that took him away from climbing. We missed him because he was more than just a worker to us. So, when he came back to our company, years later, we created a position for him as a civil crew leader. He then got an incredible opportunity to work at the railroad…once again moving on from us. Next time he came back it was like a son returning home. He had shown me, once again, what it meant to have heart. He has developed a deep and long-lasting affection for our tribe.

· · · · · · · · ·

Hustle is an essential leg of the three-legged leadership stool because the speed of the leader determines the rate of the pack. I don't know where this expression originated, but the truth of the concept is relevant and indisputable. Every year, in every industry, the pack has to move at a faster rate than ever before and it requires a leader who hustles to ensure the business continues to thrive. Dave, or to his close friends, "D-Rob," came to us shortly after high school and was quick to recognize that this cellular business might actually have a brighter future than washing cars or nailing shake on to the side of a bank building. In high school, he was a linebacker stud, who wanted nothing more than to win every game. He brought that same intensity to his job. That hunger, in fact, nudged him along to become one of the best tower guys our company has seen. And, even though he hates working at heights, he overcame that very reasonable fear and could do stuff as others watched in awe. He has a drive that owns the site and and takes pride in delivering a perfect site to every client. D-Rob loves to win, always plays for the team, and hustles faster than anyone. Because of his time "knee deep" in the mud, he understands and defends our people and the process they go through to maintain or build complex communication sites, and he does so with gusto. D-Rob continually reminds me to hustle—and while not something I easily do at my age; I do my best to keep up with him.

The three leaders illustrated above combine humility, heart, and hustle to varying degrees. Those core qualities are all mandatory if you desire to be a great leader. Many people have been tasked with leading men into difficult situations. Few succeed without even one of the three attributes. After having interviewed over one thousand leaders or people who longed for leadership, I have come to the conclusion that they humbly put the mission before themselves, they care about the team first, and they set the pace.

Indeed, there are other attributes to leadership but if you lack humility, few will honor your position. If you lack heart, few will follow you, especially in tough times. If you lack hustle, the team will not perform at any pace that sets themselves and consequently you apart as a leader.

Over the years since founding Legacy, we spent time training people who are high technology, IT-literate engineer types who are physically capable of heading up a mountain to climb a communi-cation tower, restore a generator, or diagnose a frequency problem on a radio. We do stuff that other people can't, in places they won't, and in conditions they couldn't. We built the toughest, smartest, and most capable workforce I know of. We altered the business to try and keep them home at night when our industry typically put crews on the road for weeks at a time. The people who perform this incredibly tough job display perseverance each and every day. From that crucible, leaders were formed who watched as we modeled the things learned from the other chapters of this book. The tower world is the only place where you start at the top of a structure and work your way down. The folks who advanced their way off the tower and down into management, and there are quite a few now, put their humility, heart, and hustle into action. The leadership awards and industry accolades that adorn my office actually belong to this new generation of leaders at Legacy!

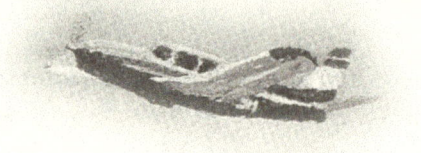

Chapter 15

Pursuit

⸻

Perseverance is an amazing quality in a person. The ability to persevere takes a focus that is not deterred by either time or circumstance. Dreamers who keep at it longer than anyone thought they could are the doers of their dreams. They can see beyond where others see with color and texture added to their vision of what could be. Everyone knows a dreamer, but how many are willing to pay the price and endure the assured long suffering to fulfill their dream? How many are willing to work harder, longer, and with steadfast belief when the obstacles are too frequent and too big? The persistent determination, grit, and resolve to persevere is a wonderful thing to watch, especially when it transforms a dream into reality.

Pursue your dream!

Virtually everyone in the world has a dream. Even children have big and sometimes audacious dreams. That's why kids can tell you with bravado what they want to be when they grow up. The famous Minnesota Viking lineman Jim Marshall, known for being the "NFL Iron Man" once told me I could play in the NFL. He could not forecast that I would top off at 5 feet, 9 inches and have my speed clocked with a calendar instead of a stopwatch. But had you asked me, I would have shared that my dream was to wear the purple and gold of my beloved Minnesota Vikings. Two problems arose. The obvious one was that I was not physically suited to be an asset in the NFL. The second one, and something I learned quickly, is that I was not prepared to pay the price that this specific dream would require.

A person's life dream is not like a bucket list. It is not something that you simply wish for. Wishes without conviction and action plans are for romantics. Dreams with plans are things that you know you are going to do. It is your personally known destiny! It is something that starts with a seed and transforms from a wish to an idea. Then from an idea, it takes root as a hope, then an urgent desire, and finally a morphing into a plan. Few can take a brash idea through all those stages of bringing a dream into reality.

· · · · · · · · ·

Noah was recently a guest on my podcast. Kind of weird because he was on one of my podcasts, not as a member of the wireless industry, but as a law enforcement officer. You see, Noah had a dream to become a cop. He got out of high school, enlisted in the military, and joined the Army as an infantryman. Soon thereafter, he became a United States Army scout sniper. Some might say this is a cool job, but it wasn't his dream. He came to work for us at Legacy and quickly became a tower lead who excelled in nighttime maintenance operations, or Night Ops, as we called them. It was a great gig, and this dude was truly good at his job when he wasn't playing practical jokes.

Noah was really creative in the practical joke department. He once called me from an unknown cell and began reading me the riot act about a misbehaving crew saying he was a radio frequency engineer for our largest customer. He led me down that path for a couple minutes, with an exaggerated accent, while I stammered and wondered what in the world was happening. Then he abruptly hung up on me. I was terrified and immediately began the information gathering process to clean up a ruined site. He called me back and told me it was a joke. I was furious, but relieved. He and the entire crew who was listening on speaker phone were roaring with laughter. We had fun together and he always did a great job in his role, but this was not his dream.

One day Noah told me he had been accepted into the Police Academy. I knew he had expressed interest in law enforcement but did not understand the depth of his dream. Taking the opportunity to sit down with him was not only enlightening, but it was also fascinating. Trying to coach Noah here was easy because he listened to and responded to counsel. It was easy to define the sacrifice that would be coming soon. Did he realize the financial strain that this would initiate? He would obviously make less money. Yes. Did he understand the emotional rigors that would become his daily life? Yes. Did he see the risk involved by transitioning to a field where he did not have depth of experience? Yes. Would he accept more money not to pursue this? No. Nothing I could say or do could persuade Noah to abandon his dream; he was committed, prepared, and ready to pay the price. Now a detective, Noah has been in law enforcement with progressively increasing rank and responsibilities for over 15 years. He is living his dream!

········

Jeremiah came to Legacy with a bachelor's degree in chemistry. Doing this communication tower technician job takes brain power, skill, athletic ability, and stamina. It does not, however, take a degree in chemistry. Jeremiah graduated magna cum laude from Central Washington University and the top chemistry graduate, but maintains he was not ready for grad school. He came to Legacy through Ryan and spent a few years figuring out life while on a tower. Jeremiah rose to lead where he proved to everyone that learning is not linear. School did not necessarily prepare you well with the ability to do tower work or lead a crew. Jeremiah was able to progress through force of will and stubborn determination not to fail. He was a great telecommunications technician, but that was not his dream.

Like many people who are tower hands, Jeremiah is a practical joker. He once greeted my wife at a Fourth of July party with a beautiful red rose. Little did she know that the flower had been dipped in liquid nitrogen. As we were arriving in the truck, Jeremiah approached, handed her the rose, but "accidentally" dropped the wonderfully thoughtful blossom to the sidewalk where it immediately shattered. He had a great laugh and continued to greet every female that arrived with this chemists sense of humor gag.

Jeremiah's dream was to put his degree to work and had been considering the Air Force. We at Legacy had no idea that this crazy scientist would even think about military service. One day, he strolled in and let us know he had joined up and would be headed into the United States Air Force. In his own words, he did not want to leave, but his dream left him "restless." Dreams will do that! Jeremiah went through boot camp and was commissioned as an officer. Since that point he has exceeded almost everyone's expectations, including his own. His wife knew he could do anything! He got a master's in chemistry and followed up with a PhD in chemistry from Montana State University. He credits life as a tower technician as a smart stepping stone to earning his Ph.D. You never know the lessons you might learn as you pursue your dream.

His dream may not have been necessarily to join the Air Force, but to use his education and serve his country. During all his time in the Air Force, he had been willing to pay the additional price that his dream required. This practical joker now responds to lieutenant colonel and doctor. He has taught chemistry at the USAF Academy in Colorado Springs for many years and now serves as the squadron commander for the Air Force testing laboratory in San Antonio, Texas. Jeremiah has been at his dream job for over 15 years in progressively increasing rank and responsibility. He is living his dream!

••••••••••

When Ryan Tracy was around three years old, my wife took a photograph of him wearing my cowboy hat and a pair of Wellington boots. I don't know when it entered his mind, but the idea that he would be a cowboy was from a very young age. When he was eight years old, the first declaration that he would be a cowboy was said to me. I smiled and discarded it as the fickle dreams of a youngster. Aside from a brief stint in grade school when he wanted to be a professional skateboarder, Ryan has known he would be a cowboy. I, on the other hand, had my doubts. During his teenaged years, Ryan spent a ton of time helping at Miracle Ranch. It was a Christian camp where the daughter of the camp director was Heidi Peterson. Her name is now Heidi Tracy and has been for over 20 years. The question in my mind was where the attraction to a ranch came from. Was it the dream to be a cowboy or the blonde hair and smile of Heidi? The answer is a resounding yes to both.

Ryan wanted to learn about being a cowboy. Immediately after graduation, he began riding rodeo bulls. At 6'1" he was not really a good candidate to be a bull rider, but it was a way to be around rodeo cowboys and learn. We watched him begin to get some modest success in bull riding and watched in horror as the bulls sometimes tried to teach him a lesson or two about the demeanor of an angry 2,000-pound animal with a strap around its middle. I chose to watch through a long camera lens because focusing on the task at hand, shooting photos, was beneficial. Once, in a practice arena the bull almost cost Ryan his left ear. That is precisely when I had endured enough. Heidi, too, had had her fill and let Ryan know that her future husband could either choose her or bulls, but not both. Whew, thank God for her stand!

Ryan and Heidi married early in life and settled into the business of tower building. In 2006, they moved to a rural town and continued building a family around a hobby horse farm. I was certain that the itch to be a cowboy had been scratched, and we would always have access to a horse to ride or pack out elk with. But Ryan's dream to be a cowboy would not be contained. Cowboys need horses to tend to cattle. In 2014, he came to me and said he would like to work late afternoons, evenings, and weekends so he could work as a cowboy. He would be breaking young horses and fixing problem horses so he could grow as an experienced horseman. I was in disbelief, my partner just told me that he had to start actively pursuing his dream before he got too old to do it. I did not yet equate cowboy and horseman culminating into cows and ranching. Sarah and I have always encouraged our kids to chase their dreams and assured them we would be beside them to cheer them on. But this would be a fool's errand. "Sure, go ahead." I told him, "We've got your back." Certain he would learn from this and hoping he wouldn't get hurt, we watched as he rode horses that clients had ruined and were paying someone else to fix. It didn't scratch the itch, the dream wouldn't die. Ryan broke horses, his nose, and both wrists riding beasts who were too rank for amateurs. For three months, he worked two jobs where the critters tried to kill him in the morning and the customers drove him hard at night.

After our first liquidity event, Ryan came back to me and repeated that he was ready to finally get into the ranching business. He had always joked that if he ever became a millionaire, he had a plan to ranch until it was gone. Now, the plan was beginning to show fruition, and he acquired a large grazing rights allotment near the Canadian border. Then he built a large training arena at his house and closed on a ranch with a feedlot for finishing cattle. I cannot begin to detail all the half-crazy things he did to pursue this dream, but Ryan is a true-life rancher. Not only that, but he is also a rare first-generation rancher who had no one in his family who had even been in agriculture. He had no mentors, no help, no bankers, and no likelihood of success. But he studied and searched out relationships with people who knew the business of ranching, those who knew about horses, cattle, land, water, feed, and virtually every other knowledge tidbit that could enable him to overcome the odds. His pursuit of mentors in any area of expertise is the stuff of legends.

Apparently, no one informed my son that if you wanted to be a rancher, you needed land. Land these days only comes from the families who hold it in trust for the next generation. They also forgot to tell him that you needed beef herds to put on the ground that you didn't have. That's key because after you have ground, you need grass. Then you need cows to eat the grass and have babies. Then you need to keep the mama cows and their heifer daughters to have more babies. All during these cycles of no income, you need to feed these critters who never stop eating, breaking fences, getting sick, and sometimes dying. Ranching is a cash flow nightmare business with low margins and hard work. I have never been gambler enough to even think about being a rancher.

To keep his dream alive, Ryan patiently learned how to acquire grazing rights, build a herd from scratch, work multiple jobs simultaneously, add margin by taking his beef directly to the consumer, and ultimately, become an authentic rancher. He enlisted the help of people who bought into his dream and the lifestyle that accompanies it. He didn't believe those who said it could not be done. I often ask folks how many first-generation ranchers or farmers they know who had zero family expertise, inherited land, or knowledge of agriculture. Their answer is generally always no one. He never let up, and he is living his dream!

· · · · · · · · ·

These three men have some things in common. They were all excellent tower hands. They led crews of men and continue to lead men today. They had every right to be satisfied with their roles and responsibilities in the Legacy family. They had great jobs with bright futures in a growth industry with an amazing upside. To some degree they never walked away from something, they all walked toward the dream. While at Legacy, they put together their plans and began the process of using their skills to plot their strategy. Their strategy became the work gloves and tools that built the dreams into practical realities. However improbable or some would even say impossible, the dreams of these three are lessons to all of us. If the hope takes root and the voice won't stop, without any promises of success, if you pursue with vigor, and yield to the chase relentlessly, you can pursue your dream!

Chapter 16

Perseverance

B eing a great coach means you must suffer through hours, weeks, and months of watching your players do it wrong. The next step isn't a walk in the park either. Now that you understand and can see the weaknesses, you, as a coach, must fix those issues, and you must do so in a way that each individual can receive and enact. Good coaching includes the constant watching and waiting for small, subtle, less understandable, and invariably more complex improvements to take hold. If I relate it to football, coaching offensive linemen, for example, may simply mean getting in someone's way. It then moves to changing the start point to be better at moving the defense away from the ball. Finer points follow that make a huge difference in your effectiveness. Your hips must learn how to stay low, and your hands need to work actively but only inside your shoulders. Then you need to learn how to make your feet obey and do it without thinking.

Great coaches add techniques both incrementally and sequentially. You soon do things seamlessly without having to message the different parts of your body. Great coaches get you to do what may not be natural to you but is required if you want to get better. It takes continual persistence.

··········

One of the most natural athletes I have ever seen was Maggie, my yellow lab. After she was killed in a truck accident, I knew I would not want another dog. She was my girl, and the hurt after losing her was far too big. I was simply done with working dogs—hunting dogs, in particular. My wife knew my distress but didn't know my feelings about replacing that special girl when she found me a yellow Labrador who was specifically bred from amazing genetics and delivered to me as a seven-week-old puppy. I was thunderstruck by the audacity of someone getting me another dog. It was neither the first nor the last time Sarah would surprise me.

So, now I had this dog I did not want, and it was a yellow lab, like the one I lost. So as not to call the new dog Maggie inadvertently and feel bad about my lost beloved girl, I just named the new one Maggie as well. For at least six months I left the new puppy untrained, and while my wife and family loved on the dog, I ignored her. Finally, after growing tired of a dog who did not know how to mind, I decided someone better get control of this monster. One way I could do that was to inquire about a hunt test for retrieving dogs. My first registration went in, and I was on the hook to at least show up. It was to be a field test with the North American Hunting Retriever Association, (NAHRA). I was entered in the "Started" category where the very first task was to have your dog retrieve a duck that landed in a pond. I had done very little training with my pooch, but how hard could this be? My dog watched as the dead bird was catapulted out of a tripod contraption and launched through the air splashing down about 30 or 40 yards in the center of the water. Maggie was told to go fetch the bird, and she released like a rocket into action. She swam up to the bird, took one sniff of the scent, raised her nose in the air, and returned without the duck. There was no way she was putting that stinky bird in her mouth! It was a complete disaster. I was humiliated!

Humiliation can be a great motivator. I knew there would be things I could learn by watching some of these other folks work with their dogs. Then I saw something I will never forget. There was another guy running a very stylish yellow lab. Her name was Hope, and her work was mesmerizing. Her obedience was remarkable, her lines were straight and true. She worked as a teammate when on blind retrieves. That is where the dog doesn't get to see the placement of a bird but must go get it based upon direction and correction by the handler. She did everything her master asked, exactly when he asked her. She responded to whistles, arm pointing casts, and voice commands. She appeared to know what the next thing to do was even before she was asked to do it. I was stunned by how marvelous this team worked together, and I just had to know more. How did they do this? How could I ever do this? How could my worthless won't-even-pick-up-a-duck dog be like Hope. How could I be like the guy who was running Hope. I asked one of the people in the gallery who the fellow with the really nice yellow lab was. They simply responded, "Oh, that's Harry." It was a start, I had a name, the guy running a perfect yellow Labrador was Harry.

I got Harry on the phone some days later and agreed to meet him at the Puget Sound Retriever Club training grounds in Dewatto, Washington. Here was a guy who was willing to train with me but only when I promised consistency and discipline. I would discover that he would invest in me and my dog only what we invested in ourselves. He would ask if I worked on the drills he taught me between training sessions and hold me accountable for my dog's progress. Later, I would come to understand that he also held dogs responsible for their performance. If you understood what was expected and did not perform, you were culpable. Harry's standards were and are very high—both for the two- and four-legged competitors who desire to train with him. Maggie and I went on to do very well at the hunt tests on many levels in two countries and competed at the national level. "H," as many of us call him, was the person who acted as the instructor, trainer, teacher, and accountability partner I needed. He is focused and driven when it comes to his sport and he led us from beginner to master of the craft. While I have learned much from others, Harry stuck with me, showing perseverance and grit. He taught me how to be fair with a canine companion while expecting their best effort every time. He has the ability to think and predict what the dog will do and what the dog's senses will tell it, what features of terrain will impact the dog's performance and what scents will affect its execution.

Harry stood beside a new handler who really knew nothing and helped me when he had nothing to gain. He also had a tremendous amount of time to lose. Basic skills through advanced and complex multi-retrieve scenarios, Harry taught them all. He handed me the keys to unlock a Ferrari of a dog and then another as he also helped as a training partner with Bumper, my next dog. He convinced me to keep trying when I went 0 for 11, failing on my first 11 tries at the senior level. Harry helped me to never give up and search for perfection in myself before asking for it from a partner. He taught me persistence!

Harry and Hope, and Jim and Maggie qualified at the 2006 North American HRA Invitational in Colorado. It was a testament to Harry's persistence, Maggie's grace, and my heart being captured in spite of myself.

•••••••••

Dan was a professional dog trainer. He helped keep my dogs tuned up and working when I had a busy travel schedule. Sometimes I would be on the road for weeks and just needed someone to keep my girls working. Dan owned a kennel and training grounds near Spokane, Washington and met my needs and the training objectives we needed to work on.

Dan was also a human trainer. He was an expert at sitting behind the handler and watching the communication sequences that led to the reason the dog was confused. He would often ask me, "Why did you just do that?" I would freeze, not even understanding what I did or did not do correctly. He would then scold, "When you did that (insert my mistake here), your dog thought you wanted something else!" Dan did these not-so-subtle corrections to enhance your memory so you would not repeat the same mistakes. He was also a dog trainer who wanted the treatment of the dog to be fair. "You keep making the same mistakes and expect the dog to perform correctly?" or "The handler's job is to help the dog, not the other way around!"

Dan was a man's man in the worldly sense. He liked hunting, fishing, cigars, liquor, coarse joking, and dogs. Not necessarily in that order. He had regrets with his children, regrets with his wives, and refused to admit that most of these were his own doing. About the only thing I had in common with Dan was dog training. Often, I would wonder if this sport would have any place in my future as it took so much time. Further, it does not take long to figure out that God has no welcome mat out in the dog training community. On an incremental basis, I would let my faith go on display to my dog friends, but never so much I would get banished. While some of the folks ostracized me, my training buddies kept me around—even with my quirks. Dan was one of the guys who welcomed me.

In the spring of 2011, I got a call from a Canadian friend to come and get my dog from Dan's kennel. I had just arrived back home, so it wasn't a big deal, but why was she doing the calling? Dan was in the hospital and was in bad shape. He apparently had a significant stroke. I jumped in my truck and drove the four plus hours to Medical Lake, Washington where the kennel was located, picked up my dog, and headed for the hospital. There I found Janette, Dan's wife, and went to the Intensive Care Unit to visit him. He was blind as far as his peripheral vision went and almost entirely blind in one eye. You cannot be a dog trainer who is blind. They found a large mass in the back of his cranium and were scheduling a special MRI for the next morning. His brain was bleeding, and they were having difficulties controlling it with medication. The prognosis was not good, and the mood was heavy. I hung around for a few hours and frankly just had to leave. Dan was angry, and Janette was discouraged. I pledged to return in the morning and checked into a hotel.

After a fitful night, I went and worked the dog early and returned to the hospital. After talking to Dan, they took him away for the MRI. I was there when the doctor broke the news. He had a large mass the size of a tennis ball located on the right rear of his brain. It had tentacles into the brain in several places, and they would be conducting surgery within the hour to stop the bleeding from the strokes and remove the tumor. Everything was worse than expected. Right before they were to carry Dan into surgery, I asked him if I could pray with him. He said, "Yes," and I mumbled some lame prayer that meant nothing to either one of us. After realizing I had not been an effective witness and before they wheeled my friend away, I told Dan that Jesus loved him and wanted me to let him know. I told him he could go to heaven if he would confess with his mouth and believe in his heart that Jesus died for him, rose from the dead, and was coming back for those who loved him. I asked Dan if he wanted to ask Jesus into his life, and he said, "Yes." It was a simple request, but he was scared and ready. I asked him if he believed and even with his impairment, he grasped my hand and said with conviction; "I believe, I believe, I believe." Just after that, they took him in for the operation.

Four hours later, the operation was over, and the surgeon was with us in the waiting room. "Dan's doing fine," he said, "the bleeding stopped, and he is in the recovery room." Then he began to walk away from us. I said, "Hang on, what about the tumor?" The doctor turned and came back to our seats. He then said, "I cannot medically explain it, we looked for 45 minutes, the tumor is not there, I don't know where it went." With that, he walked away.

Soon after that, the recovery room nurse came in and said Dan was waking up. Janette went to see him and was back within a minute yelling at me to get in there, "Dan needs you!" I ran in to find Dan fighting his restraints and screaming my name. I said in my commander voice, "Dan, knock it off!" He had pulled his IV out and was fighting the nursing staff. The moment he heard my voice, you could see him go limp. He was still in a drug fog, but then his eyes laser-focused on mine. I approached his gurney, and he said, "Don't let me forget the dream. I've got to tell you about my dream." I told him I would not forget, and we would talk later.

After recovering, Sarah and I spent quite a bit of time with Dan. We gave him a Bible, and he began to consume it with voracity. Even with his marred eyesight, he would read and pray for hours every morning. It was like he could not get enough of God's Word. I was talking with him at least twice a week, and he was a changed man. His outlook was optimistic, and his countenance was irrevocably positive. We got him lined up with a great church that began to pray with and for him. His language was changed immediately from sailor to saint, almost like he forgot how to curse. The transformation of Dan was immediate, and everyone who knew him could see that his life had been altered. One day during the summer of that year, Dan, Janette, Sarah, and I had dinner in Spokane. He invited us to their home, and he proceeded to tell us about his dream. I won't go into personal details, but Dan found himself talking with Jesus in his dream. He was forgiven for his sins, past, present, and future. He was having a vivid conversation with the Savior while under general anesthesia. He remembered details with alarming clarity and would recall colors, smells, textures, and feelings. I have no doubt that God healed Dan of that tumor to help bring the Good News into the dog world. In the summer of 2012, I had the honor of a lifetime when I baptized Dan in his home church at Faith Bible Church in Spokane. Dan and I became close friends after he got saved. We often talked about the struggles, especially with deteriorating health, but he never forgot what he was saved from or where he was going.

On May 28, 2019, Dan got to meet Jesus face to face and not in a dream. We talked about the song, "I Can Only Imagine" by Mercy Me, before he went home. On July 20, 2019, at Dan's memorial service, I related a "Tale of Two Dans." Many people in the dog world were there who had witnessed the transformation in his life. Dan was one of the last people anyone, including me, would have thought would embrace a faith in Jesus. Through my voice, Dan's testimony got the final say about bringing Jesus into the dog world. I've had no greater privilege than being used to point someone to Christ.

Dogs who perform as a team are truly a picture of the relationship with a master; it requires submission. The last eight years of Dan's life were a picture of submission to the will of the Master. He showed me what all that could look like, and I am grateful.

Chapter 17

Courage

===============

Courage is best described as being terrified and yet willing yourself to do the thing that you fear. A soldier's courage goes above and beyond what most of us will understand. It is put to voice in the Soldier's Creed:

> I am an American soldier. I am a Warrior and a member of a team. I serve the people of the United States and live the Army Values. I will always place the mission first. I will never accept defeat. I will never quit. I will never leave a fallen comrade. I am disciplined, physically and mentally tough, trained, and proficient in my warrior tasks and drills. I will always maintain my arms, equipment, and myself. I am an expert, and I am a professional. I stand ready to deploy, engage, and destroy the enemies

of the United States of America, in close combat. I am a guardian of freedom and the American way of life. I am an American Soldier.

·········

Some of the best people I've known are those who have been forced to overcome some terrible obstacle on their way to success. Major Tracy, (yes, that is actually his name, and yes, it is the coolest name on the planet) got a much worse start to life than most anyone I know. He was stuck in a seriously broken foster care system for the majority of the first 10 years of his life and without any real training on how to be a man. Born into a family with constant drug and alcohol abuse, he was raised in large part by his older sisters—all of whom came from the same place. He was high energy, needing only four to six hours of sleep a night. Foster care cannot cope with or channel that kind of energy. It takes full-on parenting, which he did not have. He was simply told to go outside and play, no matter the time. Sunup to sundown was spent running or on a bike when he had one or hanging out at playgrounds. He ate macaroni and cheese or top ramen as a steady diet. He did not eat eggs or dairy products other than American cheese and milk—gallons of milk. Sugar, carbohydrates, and milk fueled this ultra-fast machine!

On Major's first entrance into his new home—our home—on Fox Island in Washington, he looked into my office and saw the mounted head and horns of a caribou. He promptly informed me, "You hurt animals!" I let him know we harvested animals and out of respect, used every portion of the critters, even the skin and horns as art, so nothing was wasted. I was relieved my explanation had satisfied him. But Major has always been able to question the status quo and was in fact very adept at it. The kid could argue the color of the sky if he thought there was room to finesse his way out of homework!

Later that summer, after winning second place at the state goose calling contest, Maj (one of quite a few nicknames he endured) became a hunter. He also was a quite capable student and an avid swimmer. All of these helped shape him into the man he would become: a soldier.

Major began basic training at Ft. Benning, Georgia on January 27, 2012. I had wanted him to join the Coast Guard as a rescue swimmer since he had proven great strength and ability in the water. I had even gone so far as to arrange a meeting with the Coast Guard, but the night before our recruiter meeting, he signed with the big green machine! He wanted to kick in the doors of bad guys. He got his wish and served with honor and valor in Afghanistan.

Major departed basic training having also completed AIT or Advanced Infantry Training in Fort Benning and shipped out to Fort Knox, Kentucky—the same Fort Knox where all the gold is supposed to be stored. He continued training and eventually got a shot at Ranger School because he was a good athlete. I was thrilled because there were not any Taliban forces shooting at our soldiers in Fort Knox. My relief, though, was short lived. With less than two weeks' notice, we were notified that he would be heading to Afghanistan. He would fly to Europe then jump on a two-hop flight into Kandahar airfield where he would spend a day or two and then board a Black-hawk to be delivered to a VSP (Village Stability Platform) just down the road from where the Kandahar Massacre occurred. He needed to be delivered at night and without operating aviation lights due to frequent hostile enemy fire. As it turns out, this would be a regular occurrence as the VSP was right in the heart of Taliban activity.

My son served in two VSPs in Afghanistan where the typical day included exchanging gunfire with enemy combatants either from a rooftop or while on patrol. He spent 10 months deployed with Special Forces in places where soldiers wanted to spend just a week simply to get their CIB or combat infantry badge. Major saw combat with the enemy virtually every single day of his time there. From my perspective, that of a soldier's father, I believe that these day-in and day-out exchanges were and are the toughest things for our military men to overcome. God did not design our brains to see the things that our warriors saw in the sand and rock-strewn wasteland that is Afghanistan. But their eyes saw, and their brains cannot unsee the sights, sounds, and smells of war. But my son, Major, is built to overcome adversity. He has conquered hardship since he was literally a baby, and he will overcome the invisible wounds that were the result of his time there.

Major fortunately had the opportunity to call me on a regular basis. Since I was the one who chose to be awake when he was off watch, he would call between three and four in the morning Pacific time. We had many long talks about life in general and how fragile it is. He could not share much detail of what was happening or even where he was, but the conversations we had in those dark days of the Afghan war drew us together and connected us in a way that most people will never understand. Often, the call got quickly cut short because there was trouble brewing or inserting itself into their little slice of heaven. More than once, I got hung up on with gunfire in the background, when he would simply say, "I gotta go. Love ya!" That will teach a father to pray with urgency and sincerity.

My soldier taught me that courage takes many forms and can help you overcome, even when life isn't fair.

Chapter 18

Steadfast

Being steadfast sounds like it would be boring: never moving, slow, or no speed to life. It sounds like the quality of being steadfast is something akin to life spent as a bridge abutment. You just stay there while the seasons change, and the water moves around you. The ice forms and melts, the flow carries stuff around, and you just sit there. Sounds tedious, mind numbing, and dull. But, that version of steadfast is not the only version. Steadfast also exemplifies the warrior who stands up for right without a glance at what it would cost. It looks like a father defending his family, never measuring the strength of any opponent, just doing the right thing. It feels like patriotism wrapped in the ideals that built freedom into our republic. It sounds like a buglers' playing of taps at a funeral. It acts like gravity because it doesn't stop pulling and never quits. Being steadfast means, you know and stand by what you believe. Being steadfast is being certain and having the strength to resist bending to what you know would be easier. Lord, help me be steadfast!

••••••••••

My son-in-law, Ean, is a self-contained study in quiet tenacity. Yeah, I know that that sounds a lot like a contradiction, but if you knew him, you'd see that the description is accurate. Ean is a man of few words. Not that he doesn't have much to contribute, he simply is selective about spilling it out. He will freely share his opinion; you just may have to wait for it. He did not make the best choices early in life, and he spent a great deal of time looking for who he was. He was a fellow who in that young tenacity found trouble. He then, by God's grace, worked his way out of said trouble. While I do not think he ever figured out exactly what "finding yourself" means, he found his identity. His identity was in Christ. In short, Ean is not very good at giving up. I'm thankful for that.

Tumultuous to steadfast is a great descriptor of this man who has become more friend than relative. We do many things together, mostly out of doors, manly kinds of things. We shoot, hunt, and fish together. We have become very comfortable spending time with one another without talking. Many times, we just enjoy the solitude of where and what we are doing and when required, we use words. This kind of relationship would make most folks uncomfortable, not us.

Ean is also a student of things he is not knowledgeable about. If we are discussing economics, airplanes, technology, a new gun, or any hair-brained idea that comes into our heads, he typically finds the information. He is a researcher who will drill deeper and deeper until he finally understands something. From advanced technology to the newest and greatest development in goose decoys, he always goes exploring at a deeper level to solve my questions or problems.

My first memory of Ean involved thinking to myself, "Can someone please get him off my lawn?" It went downhill quickly from there. He was fresh out of one of the darkest places life offers and frankly looked like a youngster I didn't want to hang around. Without much fanfare, he one day asked if I would like to accompany him to a Seahawks game against the Minnesota Vikings. I said, "Yes," and we went to what was then called CenturyLink Field or Seahawk Stadium. As it turned out, he didn't have enough money with him for parking my truck, so I paid for the highway robbery parking near the stadium. Nearing half time, with the Seahawks holding a commanding lead, he asked for my blessing for my daughter to marry him. My strongest recommendation to young men is to take your future father-in-law to a game where his team is sure to win and not one where they are going to get trounced. The short story is that he received my blessing, one of my better decisions.

Ean is one of the most generous people I know. He is the biggest tipper to the service staff at virtually any venue. He gives his time to family and friends without expectation of any return. He once took me to a truly highbrow restaurant while we were at a conference in Las Vegas. Ean was treating me to the best steak dinner he could find. As it turned out, he chose to get me a filet mignon cut out of Japanese A5 Wagyu. The steak was around six hundred dollars, and I more than flinched when I heard the price. His heart was set on getting me that experience and while I greatly enjoyed the meal, the price alone made it hard to eat. Further, the company was a lot better than the meal.

He also is generous with his time, he fixes all my broken stuff and even replaces it when needed. I always loan things to him because if it gets broken for some reason, I know I will get the newest and greatest upgrades!

But the thing about Ean that impacts me on a consistent basis is his example of steadfastness. The dictionary would tell you that steadfast is:

To be steadfast is to be firmly fixed and not subject to change, to be firm in belief and determination, and to be loyal and faithful.

In order to be that descriptor, one would have to have it rule your actions on a very frequent basis. Ean is steadfast in the daily little things. He is careful about ensuring he stays reading the Bible every day. He is fastidious about filling his ears with things that educate and edify both. He taught me to listen to sermons and podcasts rather than fill my noggin with talk radio or sports talk. Like a few others I have met, he likes spending time with old people. Since when do cross generational discussions begin with the younger folks asking for a conversation where their primary role is to listen. Our relationship is a picture of iron sharpening iron.

Watching Ean be a husband and father is a picture that is really all you need to use as an example. He spends a great deal of time being a dad and gives those little ones both responsibility and freedom that is above their stage in life. He then gives guidance and correction that would also seemingly be above them, but is not.

Ean can execute on many things because his energies are also spent being steadfast on the little things. Thanks, Ean, for helping teach an old dog new tricks, like being **steadfast**.

Chapter 19

Valor

════════════

Valor is not courage. Most people are shocked to hear me say that, but it is true. Valor can contain an element of courage, but real valor comes when you add together honor and dignity. It is gallant bravery and strength. It can be found on the battlefield but is also present elsewhere. It comes from the Latin root word of "valorem," which means strength and moral worth. Like many of the qualities found in this book, valor begins with a thought process that swings you toward the best moral decision. To understand valor, I think it helps to envision what the opposite of valor looks like. The nature of valor is not to have your actions controlled by fear—fear of others, their thoughts, or fear of outcome. You do the right thing, which is sometimes the hard thing, but it shows by what you do. You can be filled with fear and act with valor. You cannot be controlled by fear and act with valor. Valor is often recounted on the battlefield because it is rare, it is special, and it is a foundational characteristic of a strong man.

•••••••••

Al is a guy who you can call after 10 minutes or 10 months and the conversation is the same. There is seldom much chit chat, and the conversation goes deep very quickly. How are you? Fine. How's your walk with Jesus going? Going all right, still working on my patience. Great, anything you need? Nope. See you! When there is hesitation on any of those answers, though, he jumps in with deeper questions that probe into your heart. I can't really hide anything from him. He knows me to my depths.

In May of 2014, I was fortunate and blessed to travel to Beth Shan, Israel. The day was hot and breezy. The climb up was not difficult nor steep, thanks to the nice walking path crafted for tourists trying to see the view from the top of Beth Shan. I was happy to have remembered my floppy hat and a bottle of water when I got to the top. You can see a long ways from up there, and in the shimmering heat waves, you could make out the regions beyond the military encampment of Beth Shan. My eyes fixed upon the area of the battlefield where Saul and his sons died. We read through the following passage while resting at the top of the hill, which is where the questions also arose.

1 Samuel 31, New King James Version
3 The battle became fierce against Saul. The archers hit him, and he was severely wounded by the archers. 4 Then Saul said to his armorbearer, "Draw your sword, and thrust me through with it, lest these uncircumcised men come

and thrust me through and abuse me." But his armor-bearer would not, for he was greatly afraid. Therefore, Saul took a sword and fell on it. 5 And when his armorbearer saw that Saul was dead, he also fell on his sword, and died with him. 6 So Saul, his three sons, his armorbearer, and all his men died together that same day. 7 And when the men of Israel who [were] on the other side of the valley, and [those] who [were] on the other side of the Jordan, saw that the men of Israel had fled and that Saul and his sons were dead, they forsook the cities and fled; and the Philistines came and dwelt in them. 8 So it happened the next day, when the Philistines came to strip the slain, that they found Saul and his three sons fallen on Mount Gilboa. 9 And they cut off his head and stripped off his armor, and sent [word] throughout the land of the Philistines, to proclaim [it in] the temple of their idols and among the people. 10 Then they put his armor in the temple of the Ashtoreth's, and they fastened his body to the wall of Beth Shan. 11 Now when the inhabitants of Jabesh Gilead heard what the Philistines had done to Saul, 12 all the valiant men arose and traveled all night, and took the body of Saul and the bodies of his sons from the wall of Beth Shan; and they came to Jabesh and burned them there. 13 Then they took their bones and buried [them] under the tamarisk tree at Jabesh, and fasted seven days.

Reading this passage at the exact site of its occurrence brought the pondering questions to my mind. Where did the men come from who honored Saul by taking the body of their general down from the wall?

It was pointed out that the other direction was where the soldiers who got Saul came from. I looked off into the distance and tried to fathom how they came that far? How could they have possibly done it at night? How could they have come quietly across the river and through the valley? How could they have come through the sentries and watchmen near the heavily defended fortress of the Philistine army? How did they crawl so quietly up the rocky slides to the top of the citadel wall to reclaim their general's body? How did they return via the same path carrying corpses to their own grounds for an appropriate military and religious burial? I don't know the *how* of these things because it seems so improbable.

What I do know is the *why*. They did all these things because they were loyal, steadfast, and committed. They didn't do it as soldiers, although it was a significant skill set of theirs. They did it as men of valor who loved their general. All of this made me wonder who would ever do this for me. Who would be so offended by my death at the hand of an enemy to get up, walk all night, risk their life and limb to fetch my hide from a fortified enemy stronghold? Then walk back and bury me with my sons? Who would do that?

Al would.

Alexander comes from the military. Right out of high school, he became an electronics technician in the United States Navy. He learned all the techy stuff you need to know to fix radios and radar on the run from bow to stern. He learned how to answer for stuff he did and stuff he didn't do. He honored the chain of command and earned the respect of those under his command. Al became a chief.

He was one of those guys who commanded respect and actually made the boats (submarines) and ships of Uncle Sam keep on running. Al served with dignity as an enlisted man and then as a senior NCO. After making his way to the top of the enlisted ranks, he went "mustang" and became a commissioned officer. I do not know of many who have or even could have accomplished this amazing feat of loyalty to our country through the political rigors of going from enlisted to officer. Who would do that?

Al would.

As loyal as Al was to his country, he became loyal to his faith and calling as a pastor. In typical Al fashion, he stayed cemented to one place for a second career where he served as the youth pastor, counseling pastor, administrative pastor, and executive pastor at Christ the Rock Community Church for more than 27 years. He still serves there on a part-time basis, which turns into far more hours than most people's full-time job. Who would choose to be second in command for that long of a time because they were called to service?

Al would.

Al is uncommon in this era because he values things that sound like words to other people. While I have watched him use his "commander" tone of voice and even occasionally his "commander" volume, I have not seen him be mean. I have not seen him use his considerable knowledge to belittle people even when those people might be doing really stupid things. His corrections may have either tone or volume or both but are intended to reach and to teach. They can be a rebuke that allows you or even forces you to turn away from what you are doing. He will get you to do what you don't want to do so that you can be what you always wanted. Al was the driving force behind my involvement with The Faith Mission House and the changes it brought to my life. His encouragement led me to teach at the house. His cheerleading pushed all the men and volunteers there as well. Who would commit the time to coach the un-coachable?

Al would.

Al has an uncommon level of loyalty. His loyalty is found at every level of his life. He demonstrates fierce loyalty to God, for he knows what he's been saved from. He lives extreme loyalty to his family because it is his first earthly responsibility. He exhibits predictable loyalty to command structure, even when they are making a mistake. He reveals loyalty to his convictions when he corrects the command structure that he serves, both above and below his rank. Al displays loyalty as a friend. He is a friend who will rebuke me when needed, but do so when I am alone with him so he can scold me as a true friend. He is as loyal as they come, he is my friend. I no longer wonder who would pull my dead body down from an enemy stronghold. Who would lead a pack of valiant men across the river, valley, and enemy encampment at night?

Al would.

Chapter 20

Entrepreneurship

M ost people think that entrepreneurship is something akin to trading risk for money. This might even be the business school definition, but I find it lacking in understanding. Yes, entrepreneurs continually measure risk and in the most capitalistic sense are trying to get a return on investment. Yet, that is something they do, not what they are. Entrepreneurs are the builders of dreams. They answer a call that comes from deep inside them that leads them to take risks for outcomes. The outcomes have little to do with money. Especially in the early days of the life of any business, it is seldom about money and more about survival. The dreams are not the dreams of some wonderstruck leader like Steve Jobs, but the gut reactions of someone trying to keep staff working, keep stuff flowing, and keep making payroll. It is always about the people first, the customer first, the survival first, the victory first—not the entrepreneur first. Entrepreneurs know one when they see one, because when you know, you know. It is the quality of putting others first and living the sacrifice.

· · · · · · · · · ·

There are chapters in this book about chasing dreams, building things, perseverance, brotherhood, and inspiration. This chapter is about a broader, truly American ideal: succeeding in dreams against the odds because you were built to do just that. Eric never gave up or gave in to the sometimes loud and annoying catcalls from the cheap seats that scream: "Just quit! It's not worth the pain!" But the arena seats of comfort are never where the game is played. They are certainly not ever where the game is won.

Eric is an entrepreneur in the most classic sense of the word. It is not *what* he is, it is *who* he is. If there were ever a person who embodied the notion of serial entrepreneurship, Eric is that guy. I first met him when we were exploring the possibility of connecting Legacy to other companies with the same set of standards we held. While this was not my first adventure into the land of mergers and acquisitions, it certainly became the most meaningful.

Eric and his cousin, Justin, founded Enertech Resources about the same time Ryan and I were starting Legacy. We were in the Pacific Northwest, and they were in Texas. Our business was established in a garage and a 10-by-10-foot office space and theirs was formed in a guest bedroom. We all had a great deal of need, as there were families to feed, so losing money was never really an option. I tell you these things to let you know that the things that formed me were also at work in the other people who are joined in this enterprise, and often at the same time.

Eric grew the company on an amazing trajectory. He did so by paying attention to the small details and then giving his team members the authority to fix whatever needed attention. In some circles, this style is called MBWA or **M**anagement **B**y **W**alking **A**round. I am not nearly as much of a detail guy, but I do notice things and always bring them to the attention of someone who can do something about them. He also calls this, "Management by cliché." There are many clichés that are applicable to what we do, and while most of them are borrowed from elsewhere, some are genuinely the product of this small businessman who has become a large businessman.

Eric was one of the guys who taught me to value my own model of entrepreneurship. His take is that larger organizations are slow and cumbersome and cannot capably make the quick decisions an entrepreneur can. Larger enterprises need entrepreneurs. Those quick decisions are generally done with quick risk assessment in the form of a gut check. When they pass the gut feel test, they get implemented…quickly! This type of focused response is one that you might be able to train into people, but I think you'd have to start very young because hesitation is the enemy of the entrepreneur. Yes, I place an incredibly high value on the character traits displayed by entrepreneurs.

Eric developed simple rules to follow and called them core values. His business was struggling, and he faced some choices:

1. Try to compete, by spending next to nothing on safety like his competitors were doing. He was not ok with that and decided he would rather close it down than be part of that.
2. In light of the above, he could close the business.
3. Double down on safety and figure out how to market that behavior to their customers as a true competitive advantage.

Prior to that, they were just quiet about safety. It was done because it was necessary and the right thing to do.

In typical Eric fashion, he quickly doubled down on safety training, practices, and documentation. They used this enhanced safety focus to benefit his people while differentiating Enertech from the other lesser firms in the Texas market. You know a core value because it comes from inside you. It is what you measure decisions with every single time. It is how you respond rather than how you think. How you think can be changed just like a priority can change when a higher priority comes along. We often say that if safety is a top priority, really the only thing that should change that priority is a phone call from your wife, a banker, or the Internal Revenue Service! Safety must then be a core value so if your wife, banker, or the IRS calls with terrible news, you judge your speed on the way home by your core value—not your changed priority.

I call Eric my dream builder because he had the vision to build something bigger and better so that our employees and families would benefit. He recognized the time our loved ones sacrificed while we were building the businesses. He wanted to ensure that the changes in the resulting larger enterprise would reflect our commitment to a safe workplace for our employees. He has done that and while together we have altered the business, now called Ontivity, to accommodate size, we did not change our core safety value.

Eric has begun building quite a few more companies and continues down the serial entrepreneurial road. He continues to build dreams for many people across at least four industries. Eric has, in fact, played a significant role in building my dream.

Conclusion

The process of writing this book has made me incredibly grateful. Many of the people who invested in me are not listed or mentioned. That omission certainly does not indicate they did not have an impact! It only means that there is probably a second version located somewhere in the depth of my mind to spend time on after publishing this.

The erosion of character that has become so noticeable in young men these days is not a reflection on the young people of today. It is a reflection of the lack of investment that people of influence have made in them. In short, the baby boomers, the Gen X'ers, and even now the later generations have abdicated our responsibility to impact those who follow us. Our lack of action created a vacuum, and that vacuum will be filled by whatever is in close proximity to the receiver. That could be a cold and inanimate object like a phone or video game or something living, breathing, and responding to the void. Both of these replacements are sinister because while they convey information, they seldom teach the things that are the best for someone so impressionable.

As a Grampion, a term coined by my grandson, and also as a seasoned business leader, I have witnessed how much the up-and-coming generations long for mentoring. They are seeking mentors on YouTube, in master classes, and across venues where the purpose is to take from them rather than to give to them. Before you get wound up here, I offer classes digitally, but am certain that the people who are found in the pages of these books would be proud of the content I provide. Further, I often gift them to people who need mentoring. But you are correct if you're saying the impressions would be better coming directly from me.

What's the answer? Well, it is as simple or complex as you make it. If you have some depth of experience, some qualities that reflect character, or some wisdom to share, share it. Don't share it in a format that cannot be received, share it personally! The time you take investing what you know into people who do not know will return to you in the look of joy you get when they capture some level of new understanding. When you do it face to face, they see and experience the depth of your information and the investment of your time. It may not be comfortable at first, but when you begin to schedule time with them to be spent only on them, they understand.

If you need help developing things to speak about, quit talking and be a generous listener! Then talk about what you see interests them. If you need a topic to start, just bring this book and read something not very controversial and ask them what they think. If you do that, you just found out what it is like to mentor! Then share about someone who impacted your life and begin the process of authentic and genuine engagement across the generations. These should always be moments spent building onto the character of the individual through assessment and influence.

You have great influence and the ability to share it, so turn off the phone and join someone's life by investing into the qualities that will build their character.

Then, like those heroes found in these pages, you will be building men!

About the Author

Jim Tracy is a keynote speaker, author, podcaster, and entrepreneur who has built, scaled, acquired, and sold multiple entities. He was inducted into the 2021 Class of the Wireless Hall of Fame and has served in many leadership and board roles in both for profit and non-profit organizations. Jim is a type-rated jet pilot who has trained with F-16 fighter jet instructors and also provided testimony to the US Congress.

Tracy has experienced the American dream while directing international teams, building family-owned firms, and merging companies together with strategic or private equity partners. He has been instrumental in the development and safety of the robust wireless ecosystems across the United States.

Tracy can usually be found with his wife, Sarah, and their five children or 14 grandchildren somewhere around their home in Eagle, Idaho.

Visit www.thejimtracy.com or www.thegrampion.com to keep up with Jim Tracy or inquire about speaking or podcast engagement.

A free ebook edition is available with the purchase of this book.

To claim your free ebook edition:

1. Visit MorganJamesBOGO.com
2. Sign your name CLEARLY in the space
3. Complete the form and submit a photo of the entire copyright page
4. You or your friend can download the ebook to your preferred device

Morgan James
BOGO™

A **FREE** ebook edition is available for you or a friend with the purchase of this print book.

CLEARLY SIGN YOUR NAME ABOVE

Instructions to claim your free ebook edition:
1. Visit MorganJamesBOGO.com
2. Sign your name CLEARLY in the space above
3. Complete the form and submit a photo of this entire page
4. You or your friend can download the ebook to your preferred device

Print & Digital Together Forever.

Snap a photo   Free ebook   Read anywhere